CALIFORNIA

To our native son, Nicholas — KD & Gary

CALLS YOU

CALIFORNIA CALLS YOU

The Art of Promoting the Golden State
1870 to 1940

KD Kurutz & Gary F. Kurutz

WINDGATE PRESS : SAUSALITO, CALIFORNIA

3

1925　CSL

4

Joy Riding, California Alligator Farm, Los Angeles, Cal.

CONTENTS

Art Center College of Design
Library
1700 Lida Street
Pasadena, Calif. 91103

All artwork marked "CSL" is courtesy of the California State Library.
Copyright © 2000 KD Kurutz and Gary F. Kurutz. All rights reserved. No part of this work may be reproduced or used in any form or by any means; graphic, electronic, or mechanical, including photocopying, digital scanning, or information storage and retrieval systems, without written permission of the publisher.
Windgate Press, P.O. Box 1715, Sausalito, CA 94966.

FIRST PRINTING   ISBN: 0-915269-19-8

PRINTED IN KOREA BY SUNG IN AMERICA

5

Los Angeles in 1873

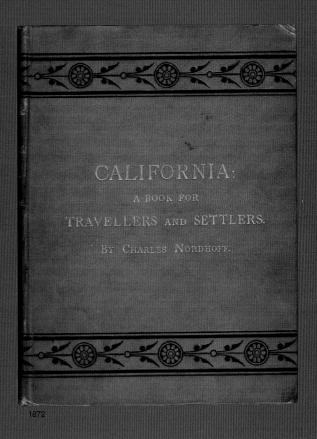

CALIFORNIA:
A BOOK FOR
TRAVELLERS AND SETTLERS.
BY CHARLES NORDHOFF.

1872

THE LAND OF SUNSHINE
SOUTHERN CALIFORNIA

1893

C205
You may throw snowballs for me.
WINTER IN THE EAST
WINTER IN CALIFORNIA
And I'll eat oranges for you.

6

Introduction

Waiting for you today in California, is more gold — better gold — than was pictured in all the dreams of the pioneers. It's the gold of great productive valleys, the mighty forests, the almost unlimited hydro-electric power, the mines and oil fields, the busy cities — the gold there is in life where Nature is always bountiful and people are prosperous.

Californians Inc., 1922

California's image has always been tied to the symbol of gold; the *golden state*, the land of *golden dreams*. The golden dreams began with the very earliest cartographers' ideas of what land lay on the western shores of the uncharted North American continent, the land of *El Dorado*. Golden dreams took on new urgency from the mid-19th century forward. For the Chinese, California was *Gold Mountain*, a land of untold wealth and opportunities at the end of a treacherous sea voyage across the Pacific; for the prospector-argonaut from Maine to Mexico, the dream was the thrill of sifting gold from the rich river banks and rocky slopes of the Sierra; for the well-to-do easterner, it was the beckoning call of travel in luxurious Pullman cars to *winter's summer garden*; for the invalid it was the promise of golden sunshine, health-giving dry air and restorative waters. For the Midwestern farmer it was first the golden grain, and later the golden orange, that prompted land-poor families to put all at risk and answer the call of *Come to California*.

These golden dreams were encouraged by the colorful language of booster literature and the captivating imagery of promotional brochures, books, citrus labels, posters and postcards that circulated to chambers of commerce, to world expositions and to friends and family *back home*. Boosters tempted potential home seekers with brightly colored images of heavily clad, snowball-throwing youngsters juxtaposed with their more lightly dressed California counterparts pulling fruit from heavily laden orange trees in December. *You may throw snowballs for me and I will eat oranges for you*, a caption taunted.

By the early 1880s, California's climate provided the most compelling reason for easterners to venture west. The booster writer, illustrator and photographer seized upon the climate, symbolized by fragrant blossoms and golden citrus, plus the intertwined symbols of gold and growth to create some of the most elaborate and beautifully-designed publications ever produced for any promotional campaign. While other states produced similar publications, none could rival the energy and success found in those of the Golden State.

California Calls You presents a selective cross-section of illustrated publications dating from 1870 to 1940. After completion of the transcontinental railroad in 1869, books and brochures such as Charles Nordoff's *California for Health, Pleasure and Residence, A Book for Travelers and Settlers* (1872), generated enthusiasm for the distant land. In southern California, enthusiasm translated into a period of land speculation that became known as the *Boom of the Eighties*. During the next several decades despite land busts, frost-damaged crops and other setbacks, California's promotional publications continued their portrayal of an abundant land of wealth and sunshine with opportunities for all. Even in the Great Depression of the 1930s, the state's apologists outwardly exhibited little of the desperation that gripped the rest of the nation. Resorts still beckoned vacationers and the roads were still open to great motoring adventures.

Publications selected for this volume represent fascinating examples of the art and language of promoting golden dreams. They are articulated in the wondrous word pictures of writers such as Charles Nordoff, Major Ben C. Truman and Edwin Markham. The illustrations convey imagery intended to dispel a vison of the "wild west" and replace it with one of productive farms and progressive communities amid bounteous orange groves with nearby breathtaking snow-capped mountains and graceful waves splashing across miles of sun-drenched beaches.

Precedents for booster imagery produced from the 1870s on can be traced to the more refined work of California's pioneer artists. Painters and photographers of the late 1860s and early 1870s, such as Thomas Hill, William Keith, Carleton Watkins and Eadweard Muybridge, recorded with such earnest skill the splendors of Yosemite, the Big Trees, Mt. Shasta and other regions of northern California, that public pressure induced officials to preserve these regions as state and national parks for future generations. To those in other parts of the country who saw the images in exhibitions or reproduced in prints and books, California's wilderness represented the ultimate goal of *Manifest Destiny*. With wealth derived from gold, California seemed indeed, the *Promised Land*. Despite California's abundant land and potential riches much of America still perceived California to be populated with rough, violent miners and too distant for leisure travel or emigration.

California's diverse topography and scenery offered compelling reasons to "see America first" rather than to visit the Swiss Alps, German river valleys or French countryside. While California's scenery could be painted in alluring word pictures and portrayed in visually gripping graphics, the promotional campaign's actual selling points remained romance, comfort and imagination. Inducements to travel west were to explore newly opened train routes in luxury, to discover vestiges of California's romantic Spanish past and to play in the *Venice of America*. This land of opportunity offered something for *everyone* — the tourist, the settler, the invalid, and the investor.

California Calls You pays homage to artists who elevated the ephemeral pamphlet to a visually arresting marketing tool. Just as artists of the gold rush era had transformed the rough miner into a mythical argonaut on canvases and in wood engravings, the image-makers for booster literature transformed arid deserts into productive farms and orchards. Further, building on the popularity of Helen Hunt Jackson's *Ramona*, writers and artists

Sentinel Peak, Yosemite Valley

8

resurrected the long-forgotten, pre-gold rush era as a carefree, romantic *Spanish Arcadia*, the last vestiges of which could be viewed in places such as Monterey, Santa Barbara and the redolent ruins of the California missions.

Several illustrated books on California establish some of the compositional precedents that influenced the imagery of promotional brochures. One of the most famous post gold rush era books to promote California was the aforementioned Charles Nordoff's *California: A Book for Travellers and Settlers* illustrated with exquisite engravings. The elegant ten-volume *Picturesque California* (1888) included work by such renowned artists as Thomas Hill. Equally handsome, *Our Italy* (1891), written by Charles Dudley Warner, provided engraved scenes to match the alluring prose of the author. Ernest Peixotto served as author and illustrator for the lovely *Romantic California* (1910). Edwin Markham's *California The Wonderful* (1914) included stunning photographs and reproductions from various artists. George Wharton James' *California: Romantic and Beautiful* (1914) also featured illustrations made from handsome paintings and photographs. *California: The Land of the Sun* (1914), written by Mary Austin and illustrated by Sutton Palmer ranks as one of the most gorgeous books of its kind. Thomas D. Murphy's *On Sunset Highways: A Book of Motor Rambles in California* (1915) showcased reproductions from some of California's most talented painters and photographers. In his preface, Murphy remarked, *In choosing paintings to be reproduced as color illustrations, I was impressed with the wealth of material I discovered. California artists have developed a distinctive school of American landscape art.* Among the artists he selected for his book were Mary de Neale Morgan, John M. Gamble, Thomas Moran, Percy Gray and Christian Jorgensen.

Works by several "fine" artists found their way into expensively produced books as well as mass-produced promotional pamphlets. Maynard Dixon produced paintings that graced the covers of Southern Pacific brochures and the company's well-known publication, *Sunset Magazine*, the Southern California Automobile Club's *Touring Topics*, the *Standard Oil Bulletin* and other similar popular publications. This volume celebrates the striking compositions and designs of the well-known as well as the obscure: Maurice Logan, William H. Bull, Arthur Cahill, J.D. Gleason, Sam Hyde Harris, Charles Siemer, Evelyn Almond Withrow, Constance Farris, and Isabel C. Martin. Further, a host of uncredited artists produced memorable images for their

clients. Even less frequently credited than artists were photographers, whose compelling black-and-white, sometimes color-tinted images complemented the descriptions and statistics used to attract travelers to the Golden State.

Writers, artists and photographers were commissioned by up-and-coming chambers of commerce, boards of trade, growers' groups and cooperatives, home seekers' bureaus, land developers, hotel and resort owners, newspaper publishers, tour companies and the powerful railroad industry. The purpose of all these efforts was, simply put, to bring people to California and increase business. Distributed throughout the country, the beckoning descriptions, persuasive statistics and beguiling images targeted wealthy tourists, successful businessmen (and women!) and industrious settlers.

Although the first oranges shipped from California were grown just outside of Sacramento, this "golden crop" became synonymous with southern California. Boosters applied such phrases as the "Garden of Eden" and "Land of Sunshine" to areas surrounding Los Angeles. Extension of railway lines — Southern Pacific's line from San Francisco to Los Angeles in 1876 and the Santa Fe's route between Chicago and Los Angeles in 1881 — became an integral part of the campaign. Writers such as Nordoff and Truman, hired by the Southern Pacific Railway Company, described in florid but convincing detail the quality of the land and the potential quality of life to be realized in these regions. The earliest publications came illustrated with woodcuts, but in time, after advances in printing techniques, publications featured vivid color lithographs. Such images graced not only pamphlet covers but also labels for crates bearing California produce to eastern merchants. Produce labels represented just one avenue for promoting California's assets through artistry and for advertising *California for the Settler* to the world.

Photography, believed by many to convey images more "truthful" than paintings, also played an important role in promotional brochures. Reacting to public suspicions that California's climate, agriculture and living conditions could not possibly match the descriptions touted in their literature, many publishers included photos and hard statistics to back up their claims. Black and white "documentary" shots of rose arbors and citrus orchards in proximity to snow-capped mountains were presented as evidence. Mechanical color-tinting contributed to this seductive vision of California giving an almost

9

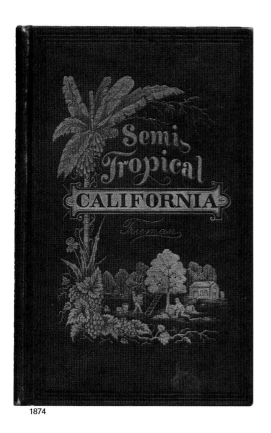
1874

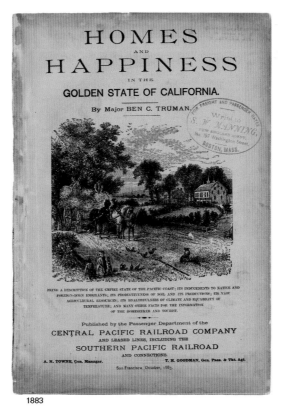
1883

1902   CSL

"surreal" tonal quality to fields of golden poppies, lush lawns and blossoming arbors.

Brochure artists of the early 20th century depicted progressive communities with petroleum towers dotting the hillsides near cozy, new homes. Belching smokestacks further confirmed the region's industrial prosperity. Delighted motorists glided through tree-shaded lanes; healthy vacationers swam, boated and played golf year-round; and care-free children enjoyed "first-rate" playgrounds and schools. To reinforce California's "modern" pace, artists rendered motor coaches zipping along modern highways, sleek aircraft streaking skyward and skyscrapers punctuating the urban landscape.

Illustrators also played their part in creating a "Vacation Land" tourist industry. Writers and artists reclaimed California's Hispanic past as a new tourist destination by showing a nostalgic picture of jolly, brown-robed padres, dashing dons and elegantly dressed señoritas. Other promotional inventions that sprang from similar roots include the *Mission Play, Old Spanish Days Fiesta* and Pasadena's enduring *Rose Parade and Tournament* in southern California. San Franciscans enjoyed the *Portola Festival*. To lure travelers and settlers to arid desert sites, boosters portrayed exotic *Arabian* oases shaded by palm trees and quenched by pools of water.

There was more to this campaign than appeared on the surface; these prophets of persuasion recorded as well as promoted social and economic changes in California. Two pieces of legislation in the early 20th century — the Panama Canal Act and the National Irrigation Act — had significant economic impact on continued development in California. Completion of the canal and massive land irrigation brought more profit and people to California than during the railroad promotions of the late 19th century. Boosters fully exploited water and trade issues in promotional literature from the late 19th into the early 20th centuries. Standing on the cusp of the 21st century, we can see the panorama unfolded and we are aware of the outcomes of this growth, social change and promised prosperity. By using the booster images as our guides, we have the advantage of distinguishing between the extraordinary euphoria and the sometimes undelivered dreams.

It is rewarding to explore these promotional pamphlets beyond their verbal or visual cliches. As attractive as most of these publications are, with their colorful covers, ebullient text

10

CIRCA 1910   CSL

1911

1931

and impressive statistics, the complex issues of population growth, economic development and social progress received little or no attention. Within the upbeat language and glowing pictures are glimpses into the struggle over water rights to support the booming southern California agricultural industry; the struggle over immigration restrictions in light of the need for labor; and the struggle over women's rights in a progressive society that promised new possibilities. The period of 1870 to 1940 revealed a remarkable evolution in projecting the California dream to the world. The title of an 1883 pamphlet promised *Homes and Happiness in the Golden State of California.* In contrast, a 1940 brochure warned: *Persons seeking employment... should be cautioned that there is no place* [in California] *for the job hunter.* Promotional brochures, while designed to position California as the best possible place to visit and live, also created a fascinating insight into the state's competing forces of progress and conservatism.

For the most part, the audience of the earlier age eagerly grasped at the glittering dreams so beautifully conceived and so well-spun in booster ephemera. These throw-away items, produced by the thousands, represented more than guidebooks

to new jobs, new homes and tourist destinations. The elements of boosterism, hyperbole and romanticized graphics can be dismissed as the glitter of fool's gold or as whitewash over more serious concerns in California's society and economy. But the words and images had great impact on all that the state has become since, and far exceeded the wildest predictions of those who created the golden dreams.

California Calls You presents the "sirens" of California's booster period spanning from 1870 to 1940. The golden nugget that initially symbolized California gave way to the golden grain, golden orange, golden poppy, "black gold," and the Golden Gate. All became symbols that expanded the imagination and the dreams of opportunity.

Today, these brochures are prized by collectors and institutions alike, not only for their visual appeal but also as a record of California's burgeoning cities and towns. They reveal better than anywhere else the Golden State's remarkable growth and transformation from a remote region to a booming, densely populated and developed state. While classed by libraries as ephemera, they are becoming better appreciated by collectors and scholars for their unique documentary value.

11

CALIFORNIA
· · ·
PAINTED BY·SUTTON PALMER
DESCRIBED BY·MARY AUSTIN

1914

12

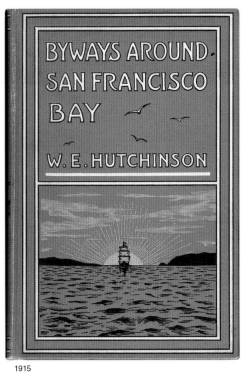

1915

1914

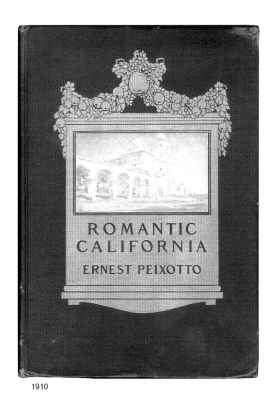

1910

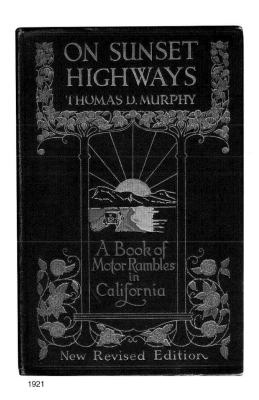

1921

1916

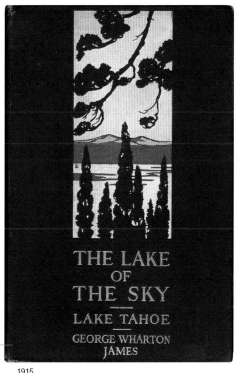

1915

13

With The Flowers And Trees In California

CHARLES FRANCIS SAUNDERS

1923

EXPOSITION MEMORIES

SAN DIEGO 1916

SAN DIEGO WRITERS

GEORGE WHARTON JAMES

1917

MY FIRST SUMMER IN THE SIERRA

BY JOHN MUIR

1911

YOSEMITE TRAILS

J · SMEATON · CHASE

1911

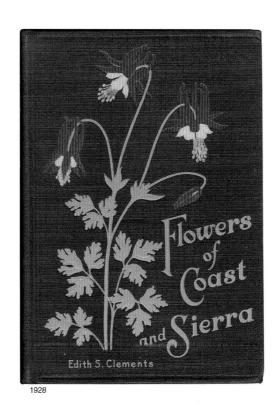

Flowers of Coast and Sierra

Edith S. Clements

1928

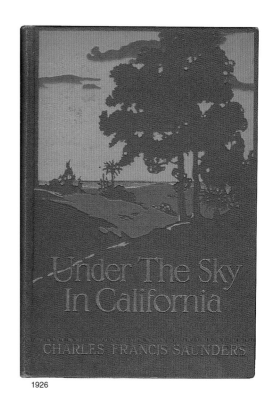

Under The Sky In California

CHARLES FRANCIS SAUNDERS

1926

14

CALIFORNIA
THE WONDERFUL

EDWIN MARKHAM

1914

VIEWS OF
❖ Pacific ❖ Grove ❖ and ❖ Vicinity ❖

ON THE CYPRESS DRIVE

BEACH AND GROVE

HOTEL & VICINITY

LIFE AT PACIFIC GROVE • MONTEREY, CALIFORNIA

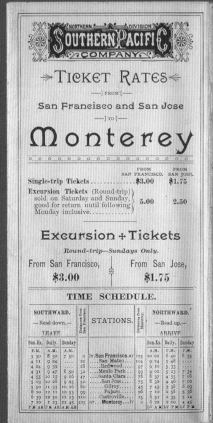

NORTHERN DIVISION
SOUTHERN PACIFIC
COMPANY

❖ TICKET RATES ❖
— FROM —
San Francisco and San Jose
— TO —

Monterey

	FROM SAN FRANCISCO.	FROM SAN JOSE.
Single-trip Tickets	$3.00	$1.75
Excursion Tickets (Round-trip) sold on Saturday and Sunday, good for return until following Monday inclusive	5.00	2.50

Excursion ✦ Tickets
Round-trip—Sundays Only.

From San Francisco, **$3.00** | From San Jose, **$1.75**

TIME SCHEDULE.

SOUTHWARD. —Read down.— LEAVE				Distance from San Francisco.	STATIONS.	Distance from Monterey.	NORTHWARD. —Read up.— ARRIVE		
Sun.Ex.	Daily.	Sunday					Sun.Ex.	Daily.	Sunday
P.M.	A.M.	A.M.					A.M.	P.M.	P.M.
3 30	8 30	7 50		0	lv.San Francisco.ar	125	10 02	6 40	8 35
4 11	9 24	....		21	..San Mateo....	104	9 24	5 48	....
4 24	9 39	....		28	...Redwood....	97	9 10	5 33	....
4 31	9 47	8 59		32	..Menlo Park..	93	9 02	5 23	7 34
4 55	10 19	9 16		47	..Santa Clara..	78	8 37	4 55	7 66
5 03	10 28	9 25		50	...San Jose...	75	8 32	4 46	7 02
5 50	11 33	10 16		80	....Gilroy....	45	7 43	3 38	6 03
6 10	12 11	10 53		99	...Pajaro....	26	7 12	2 58	5 36
6 39	12 50	11 13		110	.Castroville..	15	6 51	2 35	5 14
7 10	1 23	11 45		125	ar..Monterey..lv	0	6 22	2 00	4 45
P M	A R P	M A R					A M	L V P M	L V P M

PACIFIC GROVE
— IS REACHED —
VIA SAN FRANCISCO AND SAN JOSE
BY TAKING THE CARS OF THE

VIEW LOOKING SOUTHWARD FROM GOLDEN GATE.

NORTHERN DIVISION
SOUTHERN PACIFIC

The GREAT PLEASURE ROUTE of the PACIFIC COAST

TICKET ✦ OFFICES:
SAN FRANCISCO:
Passenger Depot, Townsend St.
(Bet. Third and Fourth Streets.)
613 Market Street (Grand Hotel)
Rotunda Baldwin Hotel
Valencia St. Stat'n

A. C. BASSETT,
SUPERINTENDENT.

H. R. JUDAH,
ASST. PASSENGER & TICKET AGENT.

PACIFIC GROVE
NEAR
MONTEREY,
CALIFORNIA.

THE PEERLESS
Seaside Resort
— AND —
Camping Ground.

ANNOUNCEMENT
— FOR —
SUMMER SEASON
1888

THE GROVE
is Open for the Reception of
Visitors, Tourists and Campers
ALL THE YEAR ROUND.

(5-88, 20 M.) CROCKER & CO'S PT. S.F.

16

1888   CSL

California for Health, Pleasure and Residence: 19th Century Promotional Brochures

*Though California has been celebrated in books,
newspapers and magazines for more than twenty
years, it is really little known to the tourist.*

Charles Nordoff, 1872

In his introduction to *California: For Health, Pleasure and Residence*, Nordoff pointed out that, although twenty-five years had passed since the discovery of gold, most easterners still perceived this western state as a land of natural wonders, human discomforts, high prices and virtual lawlessness. Certainly nothing in these unflattering images would convince the well-heeled "civilized" New Yorker to venture to California. In soothing tones, Nordoff encouraged the eastern tourist and potential settler to reconsider these "misconceptions."

There are no dangers to travelers on the beaten track in California; there are no inconveniences which a child or a tenderly reared woman would not laugh at; they dine in San Francisco rather better, and with quite as much form and a more elegant and perfect service, than in New York... Moreover, the cost of living is today less in California by a third than in any Eastern State; it is, at this time, the cheapest country in the United States to live in...

Excerpts from Nordoff's text also appeared in well-known magazines and newspapers throughout the eastern states.

Those who had much to gain from tourism and settlement in California—railroads, resorts, real estate developers, and chambers of commerce—financed production of books, pamphlets, brochures and posters. In the 1870s and 1880s, authors such as Nordoff and Major Ben C. Truman, were hired by railroad and land interests to convey in elegant prose the benefits of life in California. Several anonymous inexpensive pamphlets, meant to be distributed widely, followed a similar format. Few at first included illustrations, but in time, such publications featured wood engravings of inviting landscapes and abundant vegetation.

Promotional brochures and booster literature set the tone for "selling" the California dream from the late 19th century well into the 20th century. Nordoff presented convincing statements regarding the safety, economy and unexpected luxuries of life in California. Truman, in *Homes and Happiness in the Golden State of California* (1883), hit upon a most compelling reason to come west: *California is the only State... where a man may work in his shirt sleeves every day in the year, from January to December, and sleep under blankets nearly every night.*

Truman (and his backers) also sensed the prospective traveler or settler might not believe claims of agricultural bounty, perfect climates and economic opportunities for all. He stated: *The object of this book, unlike many others, is not to deceive, nor even to allure. The writer was instructed to "state facts and facts only."* Although this did not prevent Truman from continuing his hyperbole, he claimed concern for "authenticity" in his later material. Publishers cited statistics and presented anecdotal evidence and photographs to bolster their claims of growing economies and populations.

California's temperate climate, besides being credited as suitable for growing every kind of vegetation imaginable, was equated with good health. As Truman stated: *The dryness of the atmosphere prevents malarious disease, and is also a great relief to consumptives.* Specialized "resorts" catered to clients in search of cures for a variety of ailments. The Geysers, a popular hotel set in the midst of geothermal mineral springs in northwestern Sonoma County, drew guests for recreation as well as cures. In *Tourists' Illustrated Guide*, Truman told of a trip undertaken by writer Fred Somers, poet Charles Stoddard and artist, Julian Rix

17

PLATE—III

1. MONTE VISTA AND ANDERSON COLONIES.
2. NAPA SODA SPRINGS.
3. ROSENTHAL COLONY.
4. **CAPAY VALLEY.**
5. ORANGE CULTURE.
6. PALERMO.
7. VINE CULTURE.

DICKMAN-JONES CO. LITH. S.F.

CIRCA 1889   CSL   FROM *CALIFORNIA (OF THE NORTH)*

to shake the *San Francisco dust from their sandals... for recreation and recuperation, which emancipation they...abundantly enjoyed.* So colorful was their visit, that Somers published an amusing account of their "racket" in the San Francisco *Argonaut* of May 15, 1880. The hotel enjoyed so much popularity in the summer of 1882 that, according to Truman, the number of guests seeking rooms exceeded the number available. Men, women and children were *compelled to sleep in bath-houses and on billiard tables.*

During the 1850s through 1870s, northern California benefitted from its mineral and agricultural prosperity. Large populations and profitable commercial enterprises grew around San Francisco and Sacramento. By the late 1870s and early 1880s, promotional brochures and literature reflected a southward shift in the state's population and economic growth.

By then, claims to a temperate climate and fertile soil were more accurately applied to southern California. Railway lines connecting Southern California to other parts of the state and the rest of the country drew waves of settlers to this population-hungry area. The golden orange followed by the black gold of petroleum became the new symbols of California's prosperity. California was *The Land of Sunshine*, a title given to many booster publications. In his 1893 pamphlet of this title, Harry Ellington Brook, writing on behalf of the Southern California Bureau of Information, noted that from 1883 to 1893, the population of the southern region had tripled. He pointed to the "monetary value" of the climate which produced such valuable crops. Brook recognized, however, the need for industries other than agriculture in this booming economy. He recommended development of tanneries and paper mills, and the manufacture of cordage, work clothing and pottery. Such

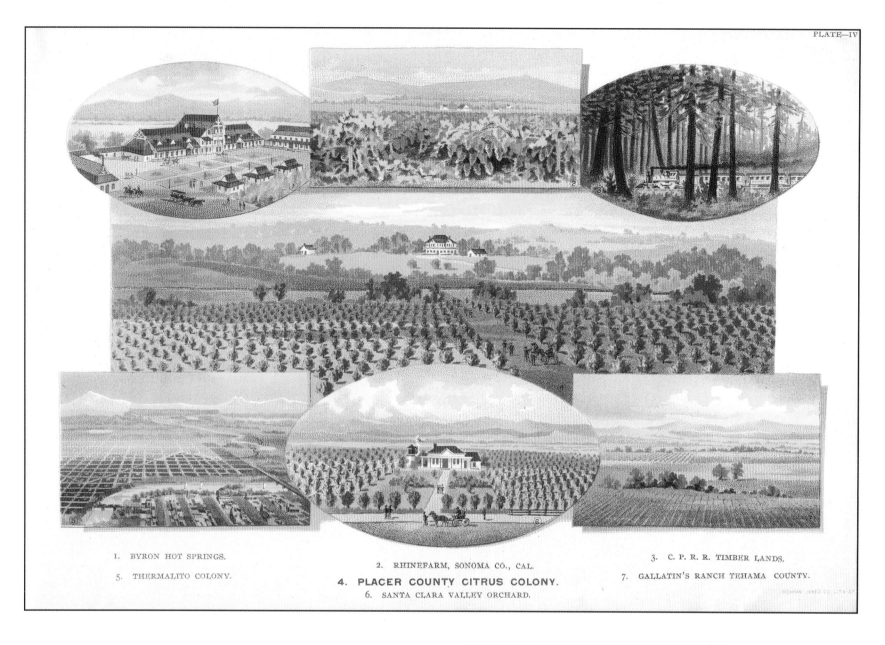

PLATE—IV

1. BYRON HOT SPRINGS.
5. THERMALITO COLONY.
2. RHINEFARM, SONOMA CO., CAL.
4. PLACER COUNTY CITRUS COLONY.
6. SANTA CLARA VALLEY ORCHARD.
3. C. P. R. R. TIMBER LANDS.
7. GALLATIN'S RANCH TEHAMA COUNTY.

literature superbly documented the "big boom" for southern California in the late 19th century.

As boosterism gained momentum, its florid language demanded equally vivid illustrations. Artists of all interests and backgrounds borrowed from prevailing styles of the fine art and commercial worlds to create visually stunning images. Posters, postcards, pamphlets and fruit crate labels created in the late 19th century set the tone and format for the advertising campaigns that continued into the 20th century.

The new century brought industrial and social progress and more reasons to appreciate California's role in shaping America's new era. But the expansive gesture inviting anyone and everyone — *either with or without capital* as Truman put it in 1883 — to come to California would evolve into more selective "targeting" of potential home seekers in the 20th century.

1. LAKE TAHOE.
5. SANTA CRUZ, CAL.
2. MT. SHASTA, CAL.
4. YOSEMITE VALLEY, CAL.
6. LICK OBSERVATORY, SAN JOSE, CAL.
3. CLIFF HOUSE, S. F. CAL.
7. SANTA YSABEL SPRINGS.

WHERE CALIFORNIA FRUITS GROW

RESOURCES OF SACRAMENTO COUNTY

A Souvenir OF THE BEE

1894   CSL

Copa de Oro
The State Flower.

CSL

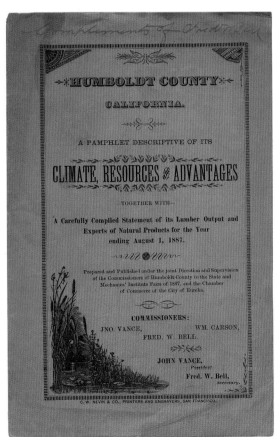

HUMBOLDT COUNTY
CALIFORNIA.

A PAMPHLET DESCRIPTIVE OF ITS

CLIMATE, RESOURCES AND ADVANTAGES

—TOGETHER WITH—

A Carefully Compiled Statement of its Lumber Output and
Exports of Natural Products for the Year
ending August 1, 1887.

Prepared and Published under the joint Direction and Supervision
of the Commissioners of Humboldt County to the State and
Mechanics' Institute Fairs of 1887, and the Chamber
of Commerce of the City of Eureka.

COMMISSIONERS:

JNO. VANCE,   WM. CARSON,
FRED. W. BELL.

JOHN VANCE,
President.
Fred. W. Bell,
Secretary.

C. W. NEVIN & CO., PRINTERS AND ENGRAVERS, SAN FRANCISCO.

1887   CSL

SACRAMENTO COUNTY
AND ITS RESOURCES

A SOUVENIR OF THE BEE 1894

OUR CAPITAL CITY PAST AND PRESENT

CSL

20

1900   CSL

1895

1883

21

SOUTHERN PACIFIC LINES IN CALIFORNIA

CALIFORNIA for the TOURIST

SOUTHERN PACIFIC LINES

22

1922

The Railroad Campaigns: California for the Tourist, California for the Settler

An organized effort is being made to attract the attention of the emigrant towards California.

Maj. Ben C. Truman, 1883

The "organized effort" to which Truman referred was that of the Southern Pacific Railway, the Central Pacific Railroad Company and the State Emigration Commissioners. He continued: *The promoters of the scheme... now have every reason to expect a large augmentation of brawn and brain to the State right steadily from this time on.*

Rapid advances had come in train travel since 1869, when the Central Pacific and Union Pacific locked iron bands across the country. When Southern Pacific opened the first route from San Francisco to Los Angeles in 1876, population and industrial growth in the state's southern region was assured. This 500-mile train ride provided an attractive alternative to the 400-mile steamer passage or the discomfort of horseback, wagon or stagecoach travel. In 1885, the Santa Fe Railway joined its rival Southern Pacific in reaching the west coast. In 1887, in the wake of southern California's land boom, the Santa Fe Railway completed its link from Chicago to Los Angeles. One year later it added a line to San Diego — *The Surf Line* — and in 1900, the Santa Fe completed a connection to Point Richmond near San Francisco. The Northwestern Pacific Railroad, formed in 1907 to serve northern California, was a joint venture between Santa Fe and Southern Pacific. Now these and other railway lines stretched throughout the state and beyond, connecting urban centers as well as rural sites. The picturesque land over which the trains traveled and the potential to capitalize on this scenery were not lost on the railroad owners.

Many promotional brochures of the late 1800s and early 1900s were written from the vantage point of the train traveler. For example, in the 1902 publication, *The Ontario-Cucamonga-Etiwanda Colonies*, the anonymous author reveled in sights

encountered when traveling by train across the *arid wastes of the Colorado Desert to the smiling landscape of Southern California... upon entering the promised land at the upper end of the San Bernadino Valley.* Supported by illustrations and photographs, he continued his heady scenic descriptions. The writer also acknowledged that this region was *traversed by all the transcontinental railroads.* He referred to Southern Pacific Railroad's Salt Lake Route *when completed,* and the Santa Fe Route which would land the traveler *in the midst of orange and lemon groves.*

The railroads aggressively pursued promotional advertising, hiring writers and artists to support their campaigns to bring tourists and settlers to California. Several railroad companies also introduced *See America First* campaigns, a sentiment echoed in travel writing from the late 19th century forward. Tourists were lured by the promise of comfortable travel accommodations, *ballasted and oil-sprinkled dustless tracks, smokeless* engines and resort destinations. These marketing ploys targeted the well-to-do, educated traveler to ensure a *socially pleasant* expedition. In the 1890s, when tourist travel to Florida was calculated at 200,000 per annum, vacation travel to California, spurred on by these railroad campaigns, eclipsed that level.

The Chicago, Milwaukee & St. Paul Railway published one of the most sumptuous brochures of its type, *California, Winter's Summer Garden* in 1915. Fashionably designed to reflect an Art Deco aesthetic, the brochure described a tour aboard *The Pacific Limited* from San Francisco to San Diego. The uncredited writer expounded on various resorts and amusements along the way as well as side trips by motor car and electric car lines.

Other efforts targeted a more "democratic" market, the potential settler, as part of the railroads' efforts to establish

23

1902   CSL

1917 AND 1922   CSL

communities on company-owned land. The settler, willing to work hard, would need land and the railway companies had extensive real estate holdings available to the investor on "term" purchase agreements. As Major Truman claimed:

[California] *has a very great quantity of new and very rich land, open to purchase and settlement at very cheap prices. This land lies always near a railroad, because every valley and part of the State suitable to agriculture is now penetrated by railroads; and the settler is able to buy cheap lands with good titles near railroad lines in every part of the State...all who would better their condition — native and foreign born — come to California and come at once.*

A later Southern Pacific brochure, *California for the Settler*, published and revised in multiple editions, had as its cover a painting by artist Arthur Cahill which depicted a strong, wholesome farmer holding a young girl with blond, curling hair in his arms. The opening section of the pamphlet read, *More Farmers Wanted*. Although the publication mentioned the fascination of orange growing, it directed its message to broader interests to stimulate diverse farming. The days of getting rich quickly with little or no capital were gone. Promoters encouraged those who

did not have sufficient capital of at least $2,500 for investing in farmland to build up their funds by first renting rooms, obtaining employment in town and by starting a garden. *Get something in the ground to live on*, exhorted the anonymous writer. Another section, *The Railroad Helping*, addressed the underlying mutual benefits to the farmer and the railroad. Improved rail facilities and equipment now made it possible to preserve fruit and other crops well enough and long enough to get them to markets across the country. The essay concluded with these bold words, *California is the land of the farmer*.

Competition between rival rail companies led to notorious "fare wars" that greatly benefitted the emigrant. So high were the stakes that, at one point, the fare from St. Louis to California dropped to $5.00, and for one astounding day, ticket prices plummeted to fifty cents. Edwin Markham, in his 1914 book, *California The Wonderful*, described this "Pullman Emigration" in remarkable terms:

Tens of thousands of tourists flocked to [the] *Far West: some of them never returned and those who did return started endless chain-stories of the beauty, the climate and productivity of California. We*

24

see the results of this westward tide of emigration in the fact that Los Angeles rose form 11,000 to 50,000 inhabitants in five years: today she has 500,000.

Railroad companies showed their interest in the land in other ways. The Northern Pacific was the first to see protection of public lands and promotion of a parks system as both a lure for tourism and a social-environmental responsibility. Even John Muir, the noted preservationist and Sierra Club founder, saw value in forming alliances with the railroad interests. Beginning in 1890, Southern Pacific lobbied on behalf of Yosemite, Sequoia and General Grant national park efforts. Through their publication *Sunset Magazine* the railroad promoted preservation. Profitable tourism, in their view, depended upon protection of these natural assets.

The remote Yosemite Valley became more accessible in 1907 with completion of the Yosemite Valley Railroad which ran from Merced to El Portal. In 1909, it joined with Southern Pacific to provide service from Los Angeles to El Portal. By 1910, passengers could avail themselves of Pullman service from San Francisco to El Portal. Rail travel, however, was beyond the budget of a large segment of travelers, and by 1915, the appeal of train travel to such places as Yosemite had given way to the growing popularity of the automobile. In 1916, more visitors used motorcars than trains to enter Yosemite Park. In the years following World War I, train travel increased briefly, but by 1935, the Yosemite Valley Railroad went into bankruptcy and within ten years the route was abandoned.

Railroad companies were not to be outdone when it came to creating tourist destinations. *Vacation Land, California's Most Accessible Pleasure Ground* was the clever and simple invention of the Northwestern Pacific Railway. Launched at the time of the 1915 Panama-Pacific International Exposition in San Francisco, the concept capitalized on the idea that the train could deliver its passengers to any number of leading resorts or camping sites. They were simply a step away from the train platform. The railway felt no competition from the great Fair, and instead, anticipated numerous *pilgrimages to Vacation Land.*

Sausalito is the door to Vacation Land... The main line of the Northwestern Pacific is now completed and in operation to Eureka....Vacationland is something more than a mere naming which an errant fancy might bestow. It is a descriptive title so peculiarly fitting to a territory admittedly unique, that, having no copyright, the name clings to this region by common consent.

The artwork for these brochures ranged from decorative cover designs and page borders to images of natural "curio-

sities" and charming landscapes. The overall look of the publications appealed to interests and tastes of the intended audience. Although the images were persuasive — vast and dramatically hued deserts, trees laden with orange blossoms, homes bordered by lush gardens, playfully-suited people enjoying ocean bathing — the texts consisted of rich, detailed descriptions of California's exceptional advantages. Often the publishers offered photographic *proof* of the state's unusual climatic conditions.

While the majority of promotional brochure illustrators were anonymous, well-known artists were employed from time to time by the railroads to produce *cover art*. This practice had the concomitant advantage of building impressive corporate art collections. Prominent among the artists were Maynard Dixon and Maurice Logan. They portrayed not only railway landscapes but occasionally indigenous populations or the by-gone era of the Spanish *arcadia*. William H. Bull, who produced artwork for Southern Pacific, created some of the most striking designs of all. His design for *California for the Tourist* — a simple golden poppy against a solid dark blue background — became one of the most effective symbols of California ever produced!

25

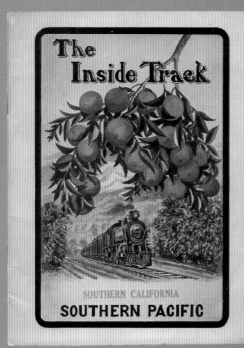

The Inside Track

SOUTHERN CALIFORNIA
SOUTHERN PACIFIC

1907   CSL

Overland Route
Lake Tahoe Line

HIGH SIERRA LAKES WITH LAKE TAHOE IN BACKGROUND

Historic,
direct way across mid-continent

CIRCA 1930

A Chain of Important California Cities

LINKED BY THE WESTERN PACIFIC RAILWAY

Substantial-Progressive- and Alive with Opportunities
ALL SERVED BY

Western Pacific Denver & Rio Grande

OROVILLE
POPULATION 3000

MARYSVILLE
POPULATION 6200

SACRAMENTO
POPULATION 71,000

STOCKTON
POPULATION 44,000

SAN FRANCISCO
POPULATION 510,000

OAKLAND
POPULATION 206,300

OROVILLE
MARYSVILLE
SACRAMENTO
WESTERN PACIFIC RAILWAY
STOCKTON
SAN FRANCISCO
OAKLAND

1914

26

CSL

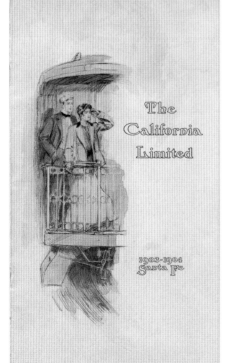

27

SUNSET LIMITED

SOUTHERN PACIFIC

SUNSET LIMITED

SOUTHERN PACIFIC

28

1913   CSL

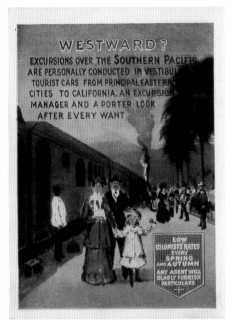

1908   CSL

1905

1911   CSL

California
for the Sportsman

SOUTHERN PACIFIC

1911

BIG TREES OF CALIFORNIA

SOUTHERN PACIFIC

1909 CSL

VACATION LAND
The PLAYGROUND OF CALIFORNIA

NORTHWESTERN PACIFIC

1922 CSL

VACATION 1917

NORTHWESTERN PACIFIC

1917

HUNTINGTON LAKE and the GRAND CANYON of the SAN JOAQUIN

HIGH SIERRAS

SAN JOAQUIN AND EASTERN RAILROAD

SAN JOAQUIN AND EASTERN RAILROAD

1920 CSL

31

Good bye Old man! We're off for California on the New Overland Limited

The perfection of traveling luxury ~ **Chicago to San Francisco in less than three days** Details from any agent of the SOUTHERN PACIFIC

1902

OVERLAND LIMITED

EXCLUSIVELY FIRST CLASS
ELECTRIC LIGHTED TRAIN
THREE DAYS
CHICAGO AND SAN FRANCISCO

UNION PACIFIC
SOUTHERN PACIFIC

OVERLAND LIMITED
CROSSING THE GREAT SALT LAKE CUT-OFF

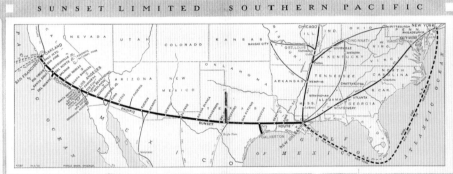

SUNSET LIMITED   SOUTHERN PACIFIC

SOUTHERN PACIFIC — SUNSET ROUTE

Conveniences on "Sunset Limited"

TELEPHONE—The train has telephone connection in Observation Car for thirty minutes before departure. Telephone calls to reach friends on train are: At New Orleans, "Main 3661;" Los Angeles, "Broadway 6796;" San Francisco, "Sutter 5920."

OBSERVATION CAR—The Observation Car contains a tastefully furnished and commodious parlor.

LIBRARY—There is a free library of latest fiction, also illustrated weekly and monthly magazines, in the Observation Car.

WRITING DESKS AND STATIONERY—In parlor end of Observation Car.

MAILS AND TELEGRAMS—Stamped letters dropped in mail box in Observation Car will be mailed at first stop; telegrams, with necessary charges, handed to conductor, will be sent from first telegraph station.

STOCK QUOTATIONS AND NEWS ITEMS are received daily by telegraph and posted in Observation Car.

ELECTRIC BERTH LAMPS— In each berth there are individual electric lamps—a convenience in retiring, or if you desire to read in your berth.

DINING CAR—"Southern Pacific Service"—equal to that of the highest-class cafes. An attractive feature of the journey, which adds to its enjoyment. The porter will inquire of passengers at what hour breakfast is desired, and they will be called accordingly.

EXTRA FARE—There is no extra fare on "Sunset Limited."

ROUTE OF
"Sunset Limited"
PROTECTED
ALL THE WAY BY
AUTOMATIC ELECTRIC
BLOCK SAFETY SIGNALS

Equipment of Train

1 6-Compartment Drawing-Room Observation Sleeping Car.
2 12-Section Drawing-Room Standard Pullman Sleeping Cars.
1 Dining Car.
1 Dynamo, Mail and Baggage Car.

Tourist Pullman Sleeping Car will be run daily between Washington, D. C., and San Francisco in connection with this train.

Daily Time Schedule
Commencing Sunday, November 16, 1913

WESTBOUND

Lv New Orleans	11.00 am	Sun.
Lv Houston	10.10 am	Sun.
Lv San Antonio	4.30 am	Mon.
Lv El Paso	10.15 am	Mon.
Ar Los Angeles	9.45 pm	Tue.
Lv Los Angeles	10.15 pm	Tue.
Ar San Francisco (Third St. Station)	1.00 pm	Wed.

EASTBOUND

Lv San Francisco (Third St. Station)	5.00 pm	Sun.
Ar Los Angeles	7.45 am	Mon.
Lv Los Angeles	8.15 am	Mon.
Lv El Paso	9.45 am	Tue.
Ar San Antonio	3.53 am	Wed.
Ar Houston	10.53 am	Wed.
Ar New Orleans	8.50 pm	Wed.

TIME BETWEEN TERMINALS

New Orleans to Los Angeles	60 h., 45 m.
New Orleans to San Francisco	76 h., 00 m.
San Francisco to New Orleans	73 h., 50 m.
Los Angeles to New Orleans	58 h., 35 m.

1913   CSL

32

They play GOLF all WINTER in CALIFORNIA

Go there by the new *Golden State Limited* running between Chicago, El Paso, Los Angeles and San Francisco over the *Rock Island and Southern Pacific Systems* Details from any Agent of the SOUTHERN PACIFIC

1903

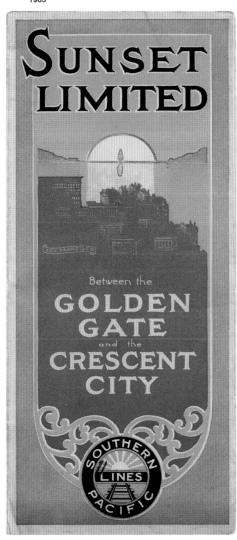

SUNSET LIMITED

Between the

GOLDEN GATE and the CRESCENT CITY

SOUTHERN PACIFIC LINES

1916   CSL

LAKE TAHOE

SOUTHERN PACIFIC

W. R. DE LAPPE

1921   CSL

33

RAYMOND·WHITCOMB LAND CRUISES TO CALIFORNIA

VINTER 1928·29

OUTWARD LAND CRUISE NO. 6

1928

1928   CSL

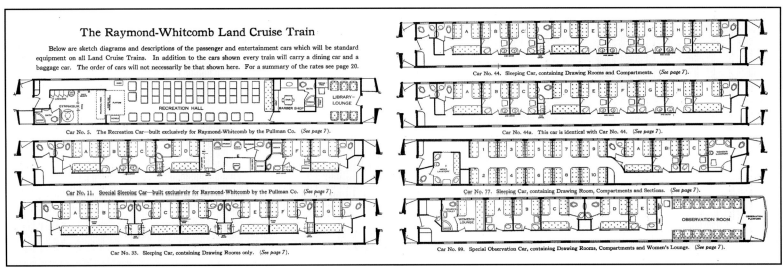

The Raymond-Whitcomb Land Cruise Train

Below are sketch diagrams and descriptions of the passenger and entertainment cars which will be standard equipment on all Land Cruise Trains. In addition to the cars shown every train will carry a dining car and a baggage car. The order of cars will not necessarily be that shown here. For a summary of the rates see page 20.

Car No. 5. The Recreation Car—built exclusively for Raymond-Whitcomb by the Pullman Co. (See page 7).

Car No. 11. Special Sleeping Car—built exclusively for Raymond-Whitcomb by the Pullman Co. (See page 7).

Car No. 33. Sleeping Car, containing Drawing Rooms only. (See page 7).

Car No. 44. Sleeping Car, containing Drawing Rooms and Compartments. (See page 7).

Car No. 44a. This car is identical with Car No. 44. (See page 7).

Car No. 77. Sleeping Car, containing Drawing Room, Compartments and Sections. (See page 7).

Car No. 99. Special Observation Car, containing Drawing Rooms, Compartments and Women's Lounge. (See page 7).

34   1928   CSL

DRAWING ROOMS AND COMPARTMENTS MAY BE USED SINGLY OR EN SUITE. THE LATTER IS AN IDEAL ARRANGEMENT FOR FAMILY PARTIES. THUS THE KIDDIES HAVE AMPLE PLAY ROOM AND OTHER MEMBERS OF THE FAMILY ENJOY PRIVACY AND COMFORT COMPARABLE TO THEIR HOME. THE SOFA IN THE DRAWING ROOM IS CONVENIENT FOR AN AFTERNOON NAP.

[14]

1924

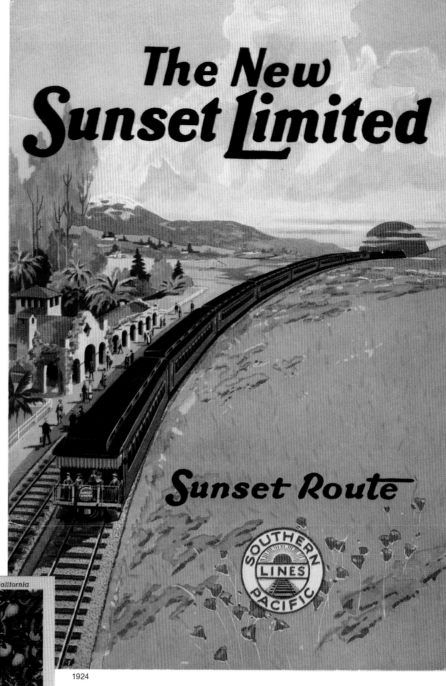

The New Sunset Limited

Sunset Route

SOUTHERN PACIFIC LINES

1924

506—Santa Fe's "Super Chief" Traveling thru the Orange Groves, California

35

CIRCA 1914　CSL

1925　CSL

1928　CSL

1924　CSL

36

MUIR WOODS NATIONAL MONUMENT *of* SEQUOIAS — **MT. TAMALPAIS** SAN FRANCISCO

San Francisco's Big Trees — The only National Park or Monument of Sequoias accessible every day of the year — MT. TAMALPAIS & MUIR WOODS RY.

San Francisco's Greatest Tourist Attraction — overlooking the Golden Gate — MT. TAMALPAIS & MUIR WOODS RY.

1923   CSL

NETHERLANDS ROUTE SACRAMENTO RIVER — SOUTHERN PACIFIC

1915   CSL

VACATION LAND THE PLAYGROUND OF CALIFORNIA — NORTHWESTERN PACIFIC

CIRCA 1915   CSL

The **RIVER LINES** SAN FRANCISCO SACRAMENTO STOCKTON — *Comfort and Luxury Afloat*

The **RIVER LINES** SAN FRANCISCO SACRAMENTO STOCKTON — *Comfort and Luxury Afloat*

HISTORICAL · ROMANTIC **SOUTHERN CALIFORNIA MISSIONS** — SAN FERNANDO MISSION FOUNDED 1797. — ASK INFORMATION BUREAU TUCKER 7272 ABOUT TRANSPORTATION SERVICE AND OTHER DETAILS — SAN GABRIEL MISSION FOUNDED 1771. — PACIFIC ELECTRIC RAILWAY — H. O. MARLER Pass. Traffic Manager

CSL

37

CALIFORNIA

The Cornucopia OF THE World

ROOM FOR MILLIONS OF IMMIGRANTS

43.795.000. ACRES OF GOVERNMENT LANDS UNTAKEN

Railroad & Private Land for a Million Farmers

A Climate for Health & Wealth WITHOUT CYCLONES OR BLIZZARDS

Rand, McNally & Co., Printers and Engravers, Chicago.

38   1885   CSL

Public Effort and Private Enterprise: California for the Investor

The striking and characteristic feature of business life in the nineteenth century, that distinguishes it from earlier periods, is the universal practice of advertising ... Of late years, it has been discovered that a city or section of country that desires to gain in population and in capital for the development of its resources must avail itself of similar methods of advertising to those used by men of business. This is especially true of a district like Southern California which is located far out of the main lines of travel through the country, and whose advantages are of a peculiar order that must be described or illustrated to be understood.

Charles Dwight Willard, 1899

California's most energetic promotional efforts were championed primarily by community leaders who formed local chambers of commerce and served on boards of supervisors. Other efforts came from the State Board of Trade, convention bureaus, Californians, Inc., the Sunset Homeseekers' Bureau and formalized women's groups. Business leaders behind each of these organizations saw California's growth linked to land investment, business diversity and solid communities. Of all the state's regions, southern California was most aggressive in marketing itself to the world and in recruiting investors, tourists and home buyers. The Los Angeles Chamber of Commerce established itself in 1888 with one thousand members to promote local development. The Chamber's campaign strategies involved advertising, product displays, publications, and mass mailings to other chambers throughout the country. Within its first decade the Chamber published some thirty-five pamphlets with a distribution to at least one million readers. Efforts to launch annual festivals faltered, but they set the bases for later successes of such events as the annual Tournament of Roses in Pasadena.

In San Francisco a group of business leaders also tried to launch a regional effort. With support of the Southern Pacific Railroad, these leaders came together in 1887 and incorporated in 1890 as the State Board of Trade with a primary goal to promote immigration. The Board represented nearly two-thirds of the state's counties and maintained offices and an exhibit space in San Francisco. Its most successful promotional effort besides its popular illustrated publications was a program called *California on Wheels*. This showcased an exhibit in railway cars which traveled throughout the southern, eastern and midwestern states. The Board acknowledged agriculture as the state's major industry and it pointed out each region's specific products in the world marketplace. The Board of Trade took credit for a slight increase in "movement" into the Sacramento and San Joaquin Valleys between 1900 and 1904.

Although nominally committed to promoting the entire state, the organization nonetheless tended to favor its base in San Francisco. In a 1904 publication, *California, The Land of Promise*, the author also presented an unusual statement (for its time) regarding San Francisco's Chinese population: *Whatever may be said of the policy permitting them to come or to stay in this country, there is now a large and wealthy Chinese population in this city, which controls and brings here... a large part of the China trade.* The link between the goal to support immigration from across the Pacific and to increase financial strength was clearly revealed in this forward thinking booklet.

The confidence expressed by this publication was almost shattered two years later when San Francisco was rocked by the April 1906 earthquake and fire. The city reawakened as a dynamic cultural and economic center due to promotional

The picturesque concrete bridge between Los Angeles and Pasadena

surrounded by the luscious grapes, the tall eucalypti, drooping peppers, and fragrant orange trees.

For more than a hundred years handfuls of alien peoples here loved, laughed and dreamed away their lives contentedly within their opulent confines.

It was the magic of gold that gave birth to modern California, although decades elapsed before the treasure wrung from the rugged mountains was destined to bless in turn the land whence it came. When the toil worn and enriched pioneers looked about for the place of their heart's desire in which to pass their declining years, Southern California was rediscovered and the

efforts of regional chambers of commerce and the State Board of Trade. Referred to in a 1909 publication as *The City of Courage*, San Francisco was determined to literally and figuratively *rise from the ashes*. The same publication stated that *three years after the greatest disaster of history*, [San Francisco] *is capable of housing the largest national, political, religious or fraternal convention*. Already San Francisco had its sights on hosting the Panama-Pacific International Exposition as testimony to the world that it was also *The City of Destiny*.

Californians, Inc., a nonprofit organization that emerged in 1922, took a more systematic approach to promoting the state. It dedicated itself to the *sound development of California... [and] finding the right man and woman for the right place in California. It is not so eager to picture California in terms that will draw myriads of people within its borders, as it is to furnish authoritative information which will assist... in an accurate measuring of the opportunities that await.*

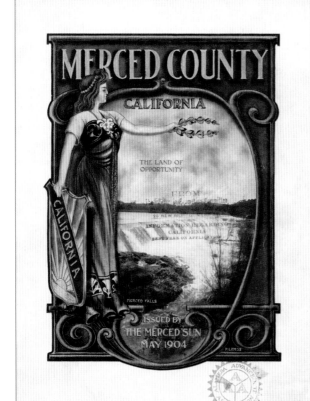

Sunny Southern California

Sunny Southern California

CIRCA 1920　CSL

41

Californians, Inc. relied on well-funded advertising tactics — letter writing, radio shows, the *silver screen*, magazines, newspapers and photographs — to ensure sound growth that translated into new highways and expanded cultural and educational facilities.

While many chamber of commerce publications were produced on behalf of state or regional interests, they provide fascinating glimpses into the life and interests of individual cities and counties. Today, they are "pocket histories" of California written from the booster viewpoint. Each brochure tried to convince readers that a particular city or county offered unequaled residential and business opportunities and, of course, a sublime climate. Most, but not all, had striking cover designs. The 1928 publication, *Berkeley... A City of Homes By the Golden Gate,* included a color cover by Randal William Borough with his equally lovely decorative motifs throughout its pages. Some brochures were formulaic, depending on stock illustrations and the frequent use of tree branches or arches to create a framed view of local scenery. Most contained short essays on every aspect of business life supported by recent statistical data. Many were illustrated with photographs intended to enhance the usefulness of these guides to the investor and home seeker.

In 1907, the Richmond Chamber of Commerce published *Richmond, The Pittsburg of the West.* Although the brochure claimed that Richmond *is the greatest city in the state of California,* the text presented other interesting facts. Richmond's relative wealth, touted the brochure, came from the *inexhaustible subterranean lakes* of oil. As a fuel source, it claimed, oil was one-third the cost of coal. The brochure made it clear that Richmond was *not* to be seen as a suburb of San Francisco. Richmond's citizens were described as working class, a *thrifty, steady, contented body of workers.* This brochure sold Richmond to business investors by describing a reliable work force and, secondarily, targeting a working class audience. It was one of the few promotional pamphlets of the day to portray workers of other races, in this instance, in a Chinese Shrimp Camp.

A 1912 chamber of commerce brochure illustrated with McCurry and Co. photographs, eloquently described California's capitol city in *Greater Sacramento: Her Achievements, Resources and Possibilities.* The author referred to the Sacramento Valley as *the garden of the world.* In addition to enumerating the region's commercial, manufacturing and agricultural assets, the author pointed out some of Sacramento's most competitive

points, that a state highway was planned to run through this *Garden of the Netherlands,* and that voters had recently approved a bond to expand its public school system. Another progressive measure was the availability of a day nursery where working women could leave their children. On a more refined level:

It is here in the beautiful Valley that the artist will be inspired by the blue skies and purple and white mountain ranges, and the towering peaks of everlasting snow, and mirroring waters of lake and stream... In this Valley the writer's inspiration will come from quaint homes, blooming orchards and fertile fields.

Promotional material of the northern counties seemed almost subdued compared to those issued by the Los Angeles Chamber of Commerce. More than one version of *Sunny Southern California* was issued in the mid- and late 1920s. As expected, the Chamber appealed to home seekers and investors with the themes of romance, flowers, fruit, climate and a superior highway system for motoring. While familiar images of languid groves of orange blossoms permeated the pamphlet, the text clearly emphasized the "go-ahead" spirit of this burgeoning metropolis:

The alchemy of progress has changed these early legends into something like reality — turned our golden summers into pageants, our seas of silver into roads of commerce... covered our plains with skykissing cities...an hundred thousand motors coasting down winding rose-rimmed boulevards through days and nights of an endless summer time... Los Angeles [is] *the busiest city on earth* [with] *a population today of 1,073,995... [and] annually 1,750,000 tourists... We are, today, the most cosmopolitan city on all this earth...*

Complementing the efforts of chambers of commerce and other groups, the *Sunset Magazine* Homeseekers Bureau sponsored a series of attractive, well-written pamphlets by various authors featuring the state's counties. The margins of the pages in the earlier editions included the dual mottos, *California Lands for Wealth* and *California Fruit for Health.* Each pamphlet was illustrated with photographs and maps and advertised the Southern Pacific Railway and its connecting lines as well as *Sunset Magazine.* Despite similarity in layout, the brochures in the series were anything but formulaic.

Women's civic groups also published a number of guides and promotional brochures. One of the most interesting, *Hollywood, California,* was published by the Hollywood Business Women's Club in 1922 with a striking cover design by Isabel C. Martin. The 350 club members were identified as business

42

1915   CSL

owners, physicians, lawyers, architects, artists, musicians and department heads. The text presented a fascinating insight into Hollywood's history and women's social and economic positions in that community. Not only were Hollywood's bank profits *the largest in proportion to any other district in the United States,* but also *forty-two percent of its shops* [were] *owned by women.* Like many promotional publications, this one stressed the importance of climate, access to ocean and mountains and the strength of local business. It gave special attention to the role of the motion picture industry in creating local financial success. Perhaps reflecting the unique sensibilities of the authors and publishers, the text made specific mention of the quality of schools, *for which reason parents bring their children west for the school season,* and the "look" of the business district, *a consistently artistic stretch of business houses lining miles of beautiful boulevards.* The message to move west and invest in Hollywood was directed to men and women alike.

The 1931 publication, *The Wonder City, Los Angeles,* provided a thorough analysis of every feature of life in southern California from homes, schools, recreation and sports, to business, crops and produce, oil, tourism, real estate and aviation. In discussing the advantages of having a home in Los Angeles, the author mentioned the opportunity to grow *flower gardens unrivaled the world over.* The author of another section, boldly claimed that water was not scarce, that it gushed through *a mammoth conduit from the High Sierra* which made *lawn sprinklers* a common feature for the southern California home.

Beyond its obvious promotional purpose, *The Wonder City, Los Angeles* celebrated Los Angeles' 150th anniversary and the approaching 1932 Olympics to be held in that city. In so doing, the publication also positioned the region as the dominant population and financial center:

Southern California has built its market according to a simple formula. Through advertising it has obtained over one million tourists annually. These tourists spend over eight million dollars a week and each 100,000 of them return to become residents and permanent consumers. Thus the tourist business causes a rapid, yet sound, transplanting of buying power from other sections to southern California — a fundamental necessity to the creation of industry here... every 24 hours, (the) permanent population increases by 222... every 24 hours, land values increase [by] *$462,196.*

While urban centers in northern and southern California enjoyed the spotlight of the world stage, central California's

43

CALIFORNIA LAND SHOW
"LAND CULTIVATION, FOOD CONSERVATION"
Our Slogan

REDUCED
RATES
ON ALL
LINES

SAN FRANCISCO   Oct. 13TH. TO 28TH.

44

CSL

agricultural interests thrust the state into the world market. A circa 1908 publication from the Fresno Chamber of Commerce read: *Coming to California? Yes! Where? Fresno "Where Farming Pays."* Targeted to both investor and settler, the text took an assertive stance:

They have heard much about Los Angeles and Southern California, and San Francisco and Northern California, but little of Central California, of the San Joaquin Valley, the vast garden spot WHERE IRRIGATION IS KING and the land as fertile as any on earth.

While agriculture dominated the state's economy, California's major concern was water as reflected in many promotional pieces from all areas of the state. Earlier promotional material of the 19th century through the first years of the new century assured potential settlers that the issue of water supply *had been satisfactorily settled in this district.* A.J. Wells, writing in a 1910 Sunset Homeseekers Bureau publication on Contra Costa County stated, *irrigation is not... required to insure crops... [but] in the next generation there will be little farming in California without artificial irrigation.* Wells also authored another pamphlet in 1910, published by the Passenger Department of the Southern Pacific, entitled, *Irrigation: California, Nevada, Oregon, Arizona.* Color-enhanced photographic collages by William H. Bull graced the front and back covers of this serious economic publication.

Whereas California's agricultural potential in the 19th century had depended in great part on the railroad industry — opening land and transporting produce to mid-western and eastern markets — the state's destiny in the 20th century as an agricultural source for the world depended upon monumental and controversial irrigation projects. For example, pamphlets produced in 1922 to showcase the northern California town of Orland boasted that it was the site of *the only U.S. Government Irrigation District entirely within California.* Another publication of the same era, *Orland, The Project of No Regrets,* published by the Glenn County Chamber of Commerce, promised that *your dream of California will come true in the Land of Orland... Irrigation development has enhanced land values ten fold... Luxurious orchards of citrus and deciduous fruits,* [testify] *eloquently that WATER IS KING and the Orland Project is still in its infancy...*

1928   CSL

45

Santa Barbara County California

Santa Barbara County California

CIRCA 1925

Where Can I Best Locate in California?

This question is being asked by thousands of people all over the United States. The answer to the question is coming back in thousands of pamphlets and pieces of literature from thousands of places, all telling of the opportunities that those localities offer.

And the information that is being given is right. For California in its entire length and breadth is veritably a land of promise, where opportunity abounds everywhere. It is, indeed, THE GOLDEN STATE.

Places of Particular Opportunity.

But the further question may be asked: Are there not localities in California to which Success is particularly beckoning, because of some happy combination of soil and climate, and by reason of fortunate economic and industrial conditions? In short, are there not in California places of particular opportunity?

Californians, and those who are intimately acquainted with the State, know this to be a fact. They know that there are in California, as elsewhere, places that offer especial inducements, and it is definite and concrete facts relative to such localities that the person desires who dreams some day of making his home in California.

1912   CSL

A FIELD OF HARDY SISKIYOU CELERY

1915 CSL

THE HEAD OF CALIFORNIA

IN THE PEACH ORCHARDS NEAR YUBA CITY, SUTTER COUNTY

1911 CSL

One of Fresno's Sources of Wealth

1910 CSL

LODGE GATE AT KEARNEY PARK

A Blue Lake Apple Orchard in Humboldt County

1910 CSL

48

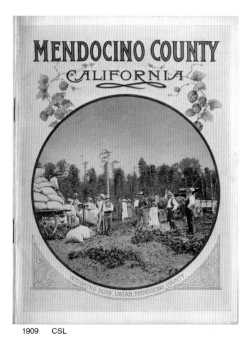

MENDOCINO COUNTY
CALIFORNIA

WEIGHING HOPS, UKIAH MENDOCINO COUNTY

1909   CSL

Fallen Leaf Lake

El Dorado County
CALIFORNIA

1909   CSL

TULARE COUNTY

ISSUED BY THE
TULARE COUNTY
BOARD OF TRADE
VISALIA, CALIFORNIA

1920   CSL

CALIFORNIA
YUBA-SUTTER COUNTIES

FEATHER RIVER, CONNECTING LINK OF YUBA-SUTTER COUNTIES

1915   CSL

BUTTE COUNTY

CALIFORNIA

BUTTE COUNTY

CALIFORNIA

1912   CSL

49

CSL

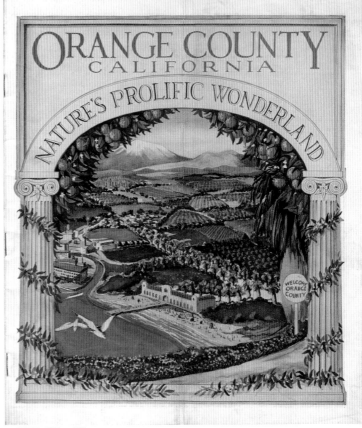

CIRCA 1925   CSL

Kern River Canyon | Kern County Sunset

50   1927-1928   CSL

1929   CSL

1923   CSL

1908   CSL

1915   CSL

51

CIRCA 1914   CSL

52

LOS ANGELES AND PICTURESQUE VICINITY.

Published by The O. Newman Co., Los Angeles, Cal.

CIRCA 1914   CSL

53

The Wonder City
LOS ANGELES

el Pueblo de Nuestra Señora   La Reina de Los Angeles

1781   1931

E.O.WITHERS

54

1925

1935 CSL

55

CIRCA 1920   CSL (above and below)

1925   CSL

56

The Virginia, Long Beach

1912

THE BREAKERS HOTEL
LONG BEACH CALIFORNIA

THE BREAKERS HOTEL
LONG BEACH CALIFORNIA

CSL

souvenir folder of LONG BEACH CALIFORNIA

PLACE STAMP HERE

Mr. F. C. & Georgia Blain
Waukesha
Wis

Municipal Auditorium and Horseshoe Pier under Construction.

CSL

57

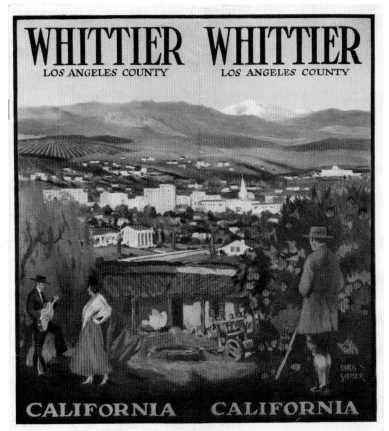

CSL

CIRCA 1914   CSL   FROM *LOS ANGELES AND PICTURESQUE VICINITY*

CSL

58

CLOSE to THINGS WORTH WHILE

THIRTEEN MILES *from* WHITTIER

FOURTEEN MILES *from* WHITTIER

Oil Wells NEAR WHITTIER

WHITTIER YMCA MOUNTAIN CAMP.

NINETEEN MILES *from* WHITTIER

In Southern California

SCENIC DRIVE NEAR WHITTIER

LOS ANGELES COUNTY California

1928   CSL

60

CIRCA 1910   CSL

1923   CSL

1923

61

CIRCA 1925   CSL

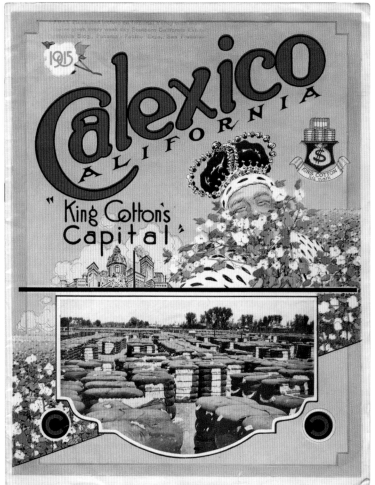

1915   CSL

CSL

CSL

62

Southern California Desert Winter Resorts — Southern Pacific / Southern Pacific

1928   CSL

DEATH VALLEY   DEATH VALLEY

1930   CSL

ESCONDIDO
THE SUN KIST VALE

ISSUED BY
ESCONDIDO CHAMBER OF COMMERCE
ESCONDIDO, CAL.

CIRCA 1915   CSL

63

CIRCA 1930   CSL   (detail, below left)

1924   CSL

1909   CSL

64

CIRCA 1930   CSL

65

ALAMEDA · COUNTY
CALIFORNIA

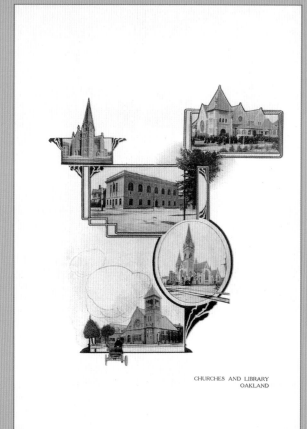

CHURCHES AND LIBRARY
OAKLAND

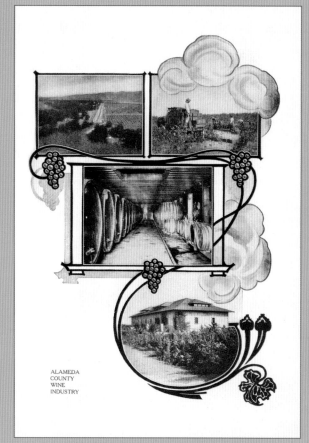

ALAMEDA
COUNTY
WINE
INDUSTRY

1909   CSL   (four interior pages, right)

THE UNIVERSITY OF CALIFORNIA

HOTELS OF OAKLAND

ALAMEDA Industry~Shipping

ALAMEDA City of Beaches

CALIFORNIA

CALIFORNIA

1926   CSL

67

1914   CSL

CSL

1923   CSL

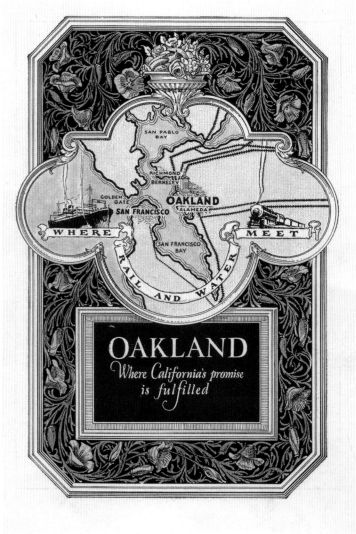

1925   CSL

68

HOTEL CLAREMONT

1908 CSL

BERKELEY CALIFORNIA

A CITY OF HOMES
BY THE GOLDEN GATE

MAURICE LOGAN

1919

69

1922 CSL

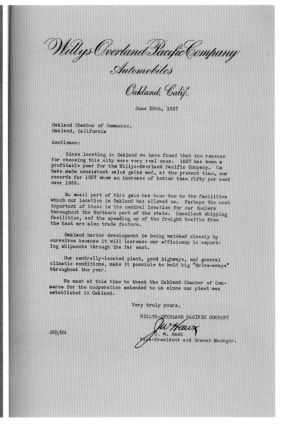

1927 CSL

1925 CSL

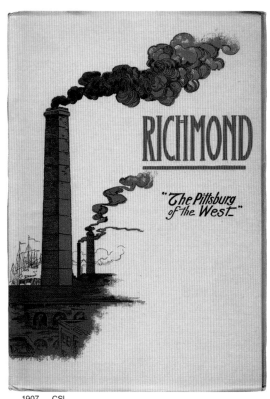

1907 CSL

70

PITTSBURG *The* BUSINESS & INDUSTRIAL CENTER *of* CONTRA COSTA CO. CALIFORNIA — Published by PITTSBURG CHAMBER of COMMERCE

PITTSBURG *The* BUSINESS & INDUSTRIAL CENTER *of* CONTRA COSTA CO. CALIFORNIA — Published by PITTSBURG CHAMBER of COMMERCE

1923   CSL

NEWARK
THE FUTURE PITTSBURG OF THE WEST

PHONE KEARNY 2798   PHONE HOME C 2798
TREWAVAS, LEE & CO.
AGENTS
26 Montgomery St.   San Francisco, Cal.

CSL

CONTRA COSTA COUNTY

1909   CSL

STANDARD OIL BULLETIN

PUBLISHED MONTHLY BY THE STANDARD OIL COMPANY (CALIFORNIA)
MAY   1925

THE INDUSTRIAL CITY OF THE WEST
PITTSBURG CALIFORNIA

1928   CSL

71

1910   CSL

1910   CSL

1915   CSL

72

IRRIGATION
CALIFORNIA, NEVADA, OREGON, ARIZONA

SOUTHERN PACIFIC

1910   CSL

PICTORIAL HISTORY OF THE AQUEDUCT

1913

1913

Engineers Inspecting Concrete Lined Canal, Alabama Hills.

73

LINDSAY

TULARE COUNTY *California*

HOME OF THE EARLY ORANGE

CIRCA 1925   CSL

CALIFORNIA KINGS COUNTY

CALIFORNIA KINGS COUNTY

1927-1928   CSL

What an Artichoke is

Reference to the Artichoke as the King of Vegetables is by no means an exaggeration. Its distinctive flavor is so different from other vegetables that one usually has to acquire a taste for artichokes in much the same way as for olives. On account of the very large percentage of iron which artichokes contain they are universally recommended by doctors and served generally in hospitals.

The Artichoke is eaten much in the same manner as asparagus. Remove outer leaves until the edible base of leaves appears tender and meaty. This portion grows sweeter and sweeter until you reach the tender heart, which is most delicious.

Try these recipes. They are practical suggestions that will add greatly to any menu. Artichokes may also be served in casserole dishes with chicken or other meats, in omelets and many other ways.

HALFMOON BAY COASTSIDE ARTICHOKE GROWERS ASSOCIATION
510 BATTERY STREET   SAN FRANCISCO, CALIFORNIA

CSL

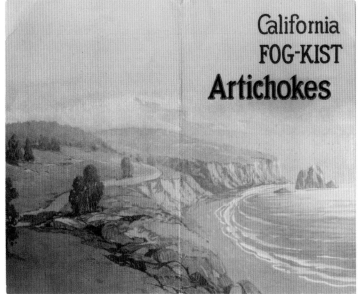

California FOG-KIST Artichokes

CSL

74

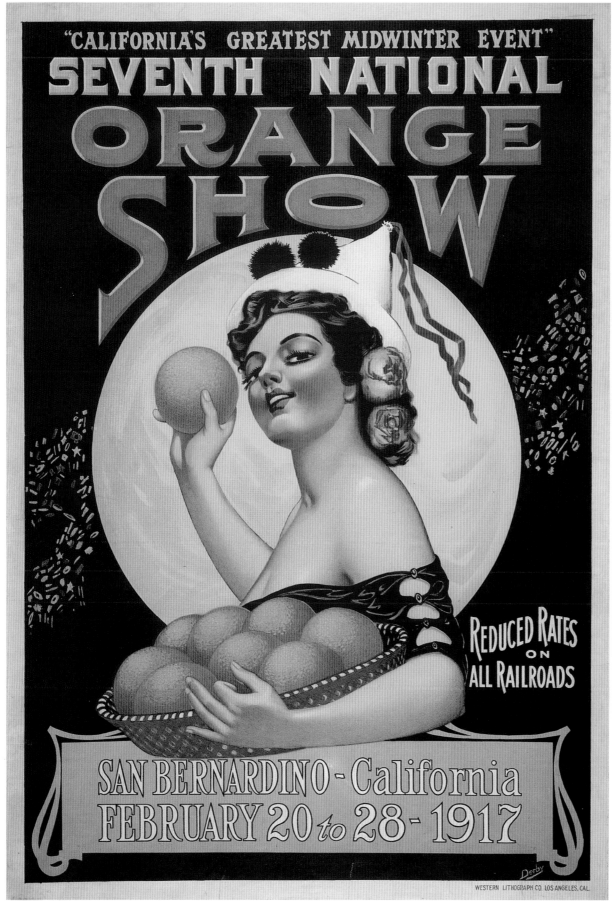

"CALIFORNIA'S GREATEST MIDWINTER EVENT"
SEVENTH NATIONAL
ORANGE
SHOW

REDUCED RATES ON ALL RAILROADS

SAN BERNARDINO - California
FEBRUARY 20 to 28 - 1917

Derby

WESTERN LITHOGRAPH CO. LOS ANGELES, CAL.

1917   CSL

75

EMBARCADERO
BRAND

Fancy
Santa Clara
Valley
PEARS

Gallagher
Fruit Co.
SAN JOSE. SANTA CLARA CO. CAL.

MUIRSON LABEL CO. S.J.

SANTA ROSA
VENTURA COUNTY LEMONS

OXNARD CITRUS ASSN.
OXNARD VENTURA COUNTY CALIFORNIA   GROWN IN U.S.A.

Sunkist

1927   CSL

RAMONA
MEMORIES

SAN FERNANDO HEIGHTS
LEMON ASSOCIATION

1931   CSL

NON IRRIGATED CUCAMONGA BLACK JUICE GRAPES

DISTRIBUTED BY
CHAS. LATIMER
ONTARIO, CALIF.

LATIMER'S VINEYARD BELT
MISSION VINEYARDS
CUCAMONGA
CALIFORNIA

MIN. NET WEIGHT 30 LBS.   PRODUCE OF U.S.A.

CSL

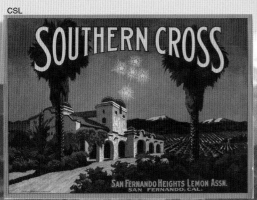

SOUTHERN CROSS

SAN FERNANDO HEIGHTS LEMON ASSN.
SAN FERNANDO, CAL.

CSL

SUNNY COVE

PURE GOLD

PACKED BY
REDLANDS FOOTHILL GROVES
REDLANDS, CALIFORNIA

GROWN IN U.S.A.

VALLEY VIEW
BRAND

W. J. WILSON & SON, Inc.

FANCY MOUNTAIN FRUIT   Newcastle, California

CSL

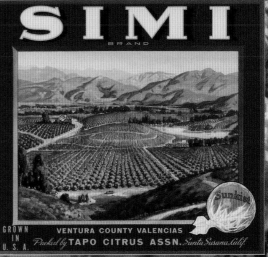

SIMI
BRAND

GROWN
IN
U.S.A.   VENTURA COUNTY VALENCIAS
Packed by TAPO CITRUS ASSN. Santa Susana, Calif.

Sunkist

CSL

77

WATSONVILLE in The Valley of the Apple

Pajaro Valley Santa Cruz County California.

1925   CSL

GRIDLEY

IN THE FEATHER RIVER
□□ PEACH BELT □□

BUTTE COUNTY
CALIFORNIA

CIRCA 1925   CSL

THE FROSTLESS BELT

ISSUED BY THE
ANAHEIM BOARD OF TRADE
ANAHEIM, CALIFORNIA

1915   CSL

The Italy OF CALIFORNIA

HEAD OF STONEY CREEK

BY FRANK FREEMAN

ORLAND THE CAPITAL

1900   CSL

LODI
CALIFORNIA

THE PERFECT FLAME TOKAY GRAPE

1913   CSL

GLENN COUNTY
CALIFORNIA

GLENN COUNTY ORANGES ARE OF EXCELLENT QUALITY

1914   CSL

SEBASTOPOL
The home of the Gravenstein

SONOMA COUNTY
CALIFORNIA

1924   CSL

Petaluma

CALIFORNIA

SOME OF THE MEN, AND THEIR FINE BRED STOCK, WHO HAVE HELPED MAKE PETALUMA'S WORLD-WIDE REPUTATION THAT "PETALUMA CHICKENS PRODUCE MORE AND BETTER EGGS." ABOVE (LEFT) WALTER HOGAN.   CENTER (RIGHT) P. R. LYDING.   LOWER (LEFT)—KNOX BOUDE.

PETALUMA PETALUMA

SONOMA COUNTY CALIFORNIA

THE WORLDS EGG-BASKET

CIRCA 1920   CSL

Just a Few Words About Chickens

 HERE are many thousands of people in the United States who are dreaming of some day owning a poultry ranch. It is well, therefore, that we mention here a few of the elements that have entered into the making of Sonoma County, the chicken raising center of this country. Sonoma County's climate seems to have been made to order for the poultryman. Transportation facilities are such as to put the poultry raising center into quick connection with great markets. The Petaluma District is the best known in the county, and the world for that matter. Here is a single marketing center where $10,000 is paid out every day in the year for poultry products. There is no reliable "chicken census" but experts agree that there are at least 4,000,000 chickens on the ranches in Sonoma County. The average egg production is 175 per hen, although 200 is common. But poultry raising is one of the least of the resources of Sonoma County. Our booklet will tell you how the farmer and the horticulturist make big money. A letter to either of the undersigned organizations will bring you further information.

A Petaluma Lay

CIRCA 1905   CSL

81

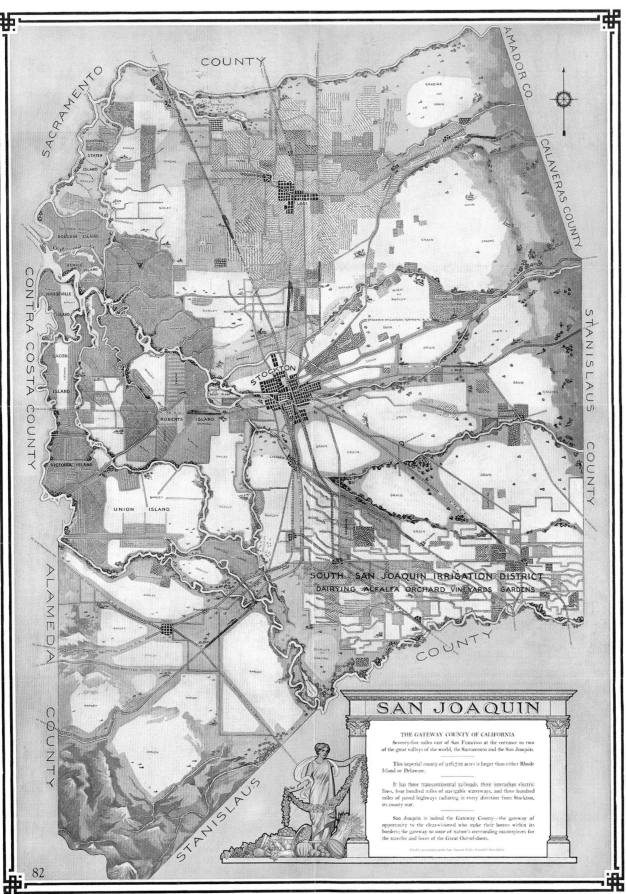

SOUTH SAN JOAQUIN IRRIGATION DISTRICT
DAIRYING ALFALFA ORCHARD VINEYARDS GARDENS

SAN JOAQUIN

THE GATEWAY COUNTY OF CALIFORNIA
Seventy-five miles east of San Francisco at the entrance to two of the great valleys of the world, the Sacramento and the San Joaquin.

This imperial county of 926,720 acres is larger than either Rhode Island or Delaware.

It has three transcontinental railroads, three interurban electric lines, four hundred miles of navigable waterways, and three hundred miles of paved highways radiating in every direction from Stockton, its county seat.

San Joaquin is indeed the Gateway County—the gateway of opportunity to the clear-visioned who make their homes within its borders; the gateway to some of nature's outstanding masterpieces for the traveler and lover of the Great Out-of-doors.

Used by permission of the San Joaquin Valley Counties' Association

82

SAN JOAQUIN COUNTY CALIFORNIA

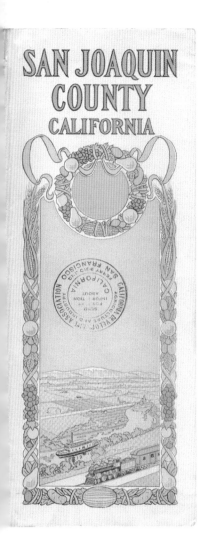

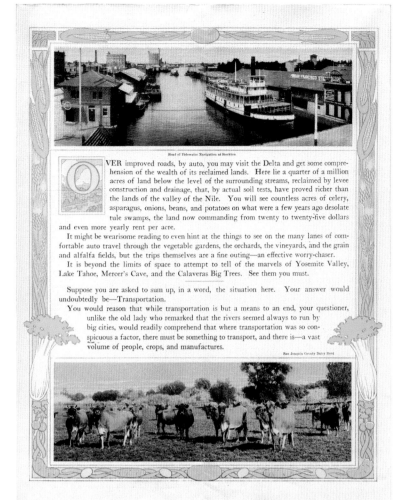

OVER improved roads, by auto, you may visit the Delta and get some comprehension of the wealth of its reclaimed lands. Here lie a quarter of a million acres of land below the level of the surrounding streams, reclaimed by levee construction and drainage, that, by actual soil tests, have proved richer than the lands of the valley of the Nile. You will see countless acres of celery, asparagus, onions, beans, and potatoes on what were a few years ago desolate tule swamps, the land now commanding from twenty to twenty-five dollars and even more yearly rent per acre.

It might be wearisome reading to even hint at the things to see on the many lanes of comfortable auto travel through the vegetable gardens, the orchards, the vineyards, and the grain and alfalfa fields, but the trips themselves are a fine outing—an effective worry-chaser.

It is beyond the limits of space to attempt to tell of the marvels of Yosemite Valley, Lake Tahoe, Mercer's Cave, and the Calaveras Big Trees. See them you must.

Suppose you are asked to sum up, in a word, the situation here. Your answer would undoubtedly be—Transportation.

You would reason that while transportation is but a means to an end, your questioner, unlike the old lady who remarked that the rivers seemed always to run by big cities, would readily comprehend that where transportation was so conspicuous a factor, there must be something to transport, and there is—a vast volume of people, crops, and manufactures.

1915   CSL

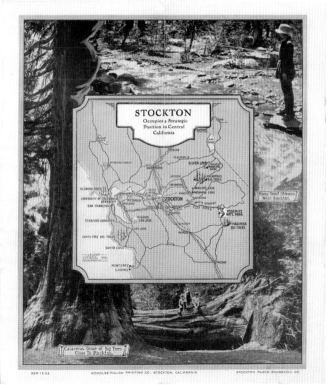

1923   CSL

1923   CSL

83

Thermalito Colony

THE PASADENA OF CENTRAL CALIFORNIA

ADDRESS Thermalito Colony Co.,
A CORPORATION

OROVILLE, BUTTE Co.

OR MIDDLETON & SHARON, 22 Montgomery St. S.F.

OR SEWELL & WELTON, Sacramento, Cal.

4016

MAP OF THERMALITO BUTTE COUNTY CALIFORNIA

GROUNDS OF BUTTE CO INFIRMARY.

OROVILLE

FEATHER RIVER

PRIVATE LAND 160 ACRES

SCHMIDT LABEL & LITH CO. S.F.

1887   CSL

Developers

The Basis of California's Invitation... is, first of all, room... it is inevitable that the State will become the home of a great number of people, one class coming for profit... one chiefly for farms and homes.

California for The Settler, 1917

Many who came to California from the 1880s onward looked to the land for their profit by creating communities for potential residents. Elaborate brochures produced by land developers and real estate companies often included maps, price lists and terms of sale, as well as enticing artist-drawn concepts of new and future communities. In an amusing play on the state's geography, the investors behind *Thermalito Colony* promoted their property as *The Pasadena of Central California*. Actually, Thermalito was located in Butte county, at the northern terminus of the Northern California Railroad. Terms of sale required one-third cash at the time of purchase; one-third in the following year; and the balance in the third year. Free water was offered to all purchasers.

Publications produced by real estate developers recognized a desire for year-round homes, not just vacation homes, in idyllic settings, away from the confines of densely populated cities. These brochures articulated the emergence of a phenomenon made famous in southern California — suburbia. One southern California development, *Palm Place*, hoped to entice *men of wealth or leisure... seeking the freedom and seclusion of suburban home life, where the very spaciousness permits each member of the family to develop greater individuality.* The villa lots for this planned community were designed by landscape architect Wilbur David Cook. A sumptuous 1905 brochure announced *Naples, An Artistic Dream and Its Realization.* Watercolor drawings by D.F. Schwartz showed exotic buildings in *Moorish, Venetian* and *Neapolitan* styles along romantic man-made canals that led to the sea.

In 1910, *Claremont*, a private *Residence Park* located near Berkeley demonstrated that the private home, located in proximity to scenic wonders, yet not distant from an urban center, could be within the financial reach of the "average" buyer. The promotional pamphlet, graced with drawings by William H. Bull, indicated that this elegant community was designed for *any man of moderate means... in a community where beauty and the rights of a home are a common goal.*

Promotional materials in this category reflect interests of the sellers and their intended buyers as well as complex relationships between the business interests of already existing communities. Some developers, for example, were clearly out to create "instant cities," others to build on established assets within the region. These publications, with their variety of sales pitches, document California's volatile land market through boom and bust.

85

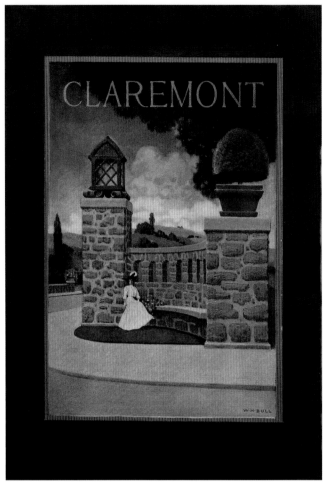

1910   CSL

1910   CSL

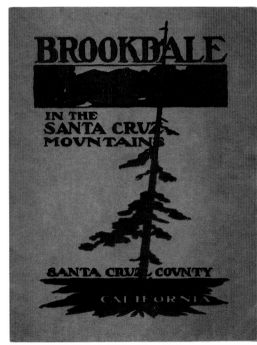

CSL

1909

86

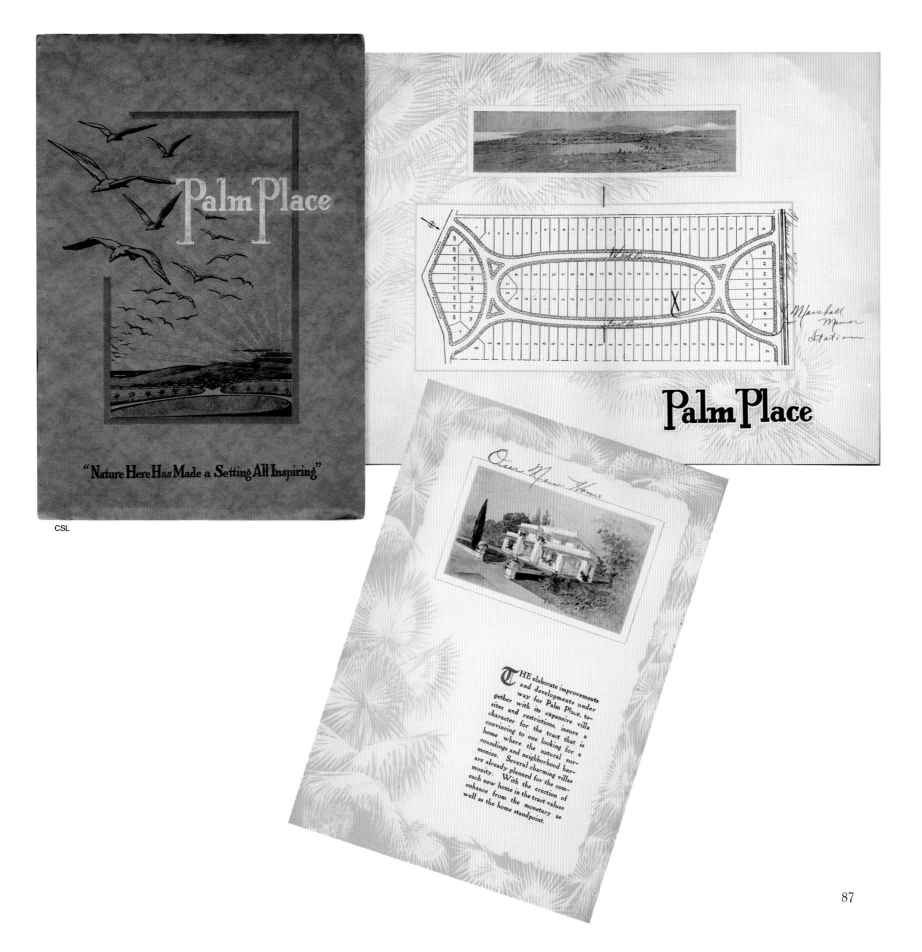

Palm Place

"Nature Here Has Made a Setting All Inspiring"

CSL

Palm Place

Our New Home

THE elaborate improvements and developments under way for Palm Place, together with its expansive villa sites and restrictions, insure a character for the tract that is convincing to one looking for a home where the natural surroundings and neighborhood harmonize. Several charming villas are already planned for the community. With the erection of each new home in the tract values enhance from the monetary as well as the home standpoint.

87

HOLLYWOOD HOLLYWOOD

1922

1923

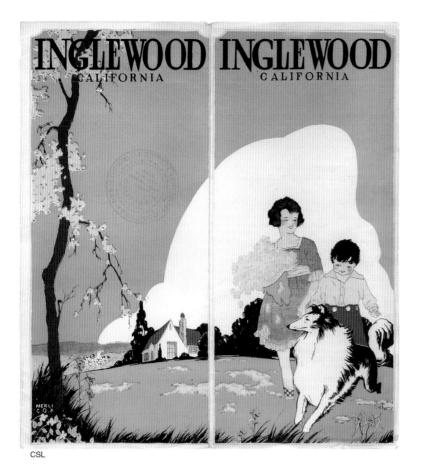

CSL

1924   CSL

1924   CSL

CSL

THE CITY
OF RED TILED ROOFS

THIS UNIQUE CONCEPTION
STANDS ALONE

Indescribably quaint, and artistic to a
degree will be the composite effect
of all the various original and
striking features of Naples,
the whole crowned by
red tiled roofs on
every build-
ing

Moorish
Venetian
Neapolitan

A trin-
ity repsesent-
ing architectural
achievements that have
never been equaled. Naples
will reproduce in a dignified and
stately manner many of the beautiful
and artistic embellishments of each one

1905   CSL (above and right)

One of Five Bridges Spanning Rivo-Alto Canal.

Naples by Moonlight.

90

NAPLES

AN ARTISTIC DREAM AND ITS REALIZATION

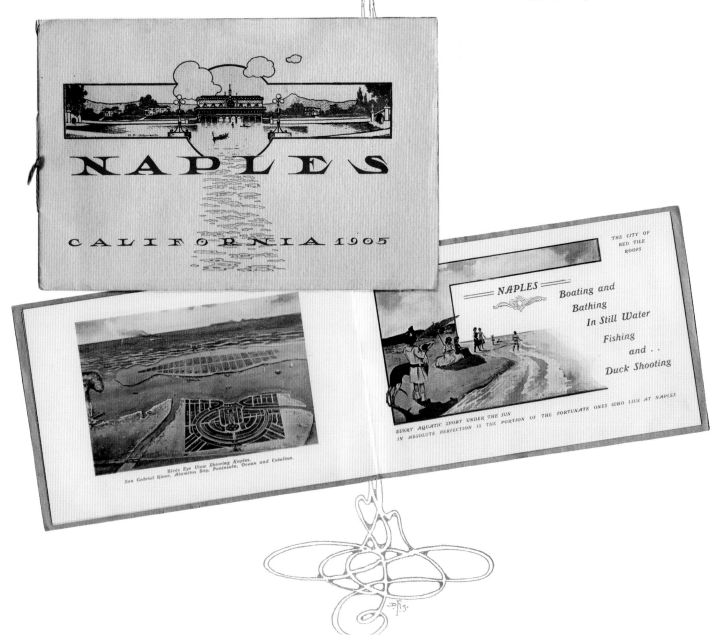

Amusements in Venice

WINDWARD AVE
THE AUDITORIUM
THE MIDWAY
PALM GARDEN

1909   CSL

Venice of America

AN EVERYDAY SCENE ON THE BEACH AT VENICE.

1922

92

1914

VENICE LIFE GUARDS

1922

SOME VENICE APARTMENT HOUSES

1922

93

The Last of the Beaches

PALISADES DEL REY

PALISADES DEL REY

Dickinson & Gillespie Co. Los Angeles

Dickinson & Gillespie Co.

SANTA MONICA AND OCEAN PARK

THE FAMOUS RESORTS OF SOUTHERN CALIFORNIA

The Temperature Here Today Is

Place Two Cent Stamp Here

SANTA MONICA AND OCEAN PARK

THE FAMOUS RESORTS OF SOUTHERN CALIFORNIA

NO SALOONS

CSL

CSL

CSL

94

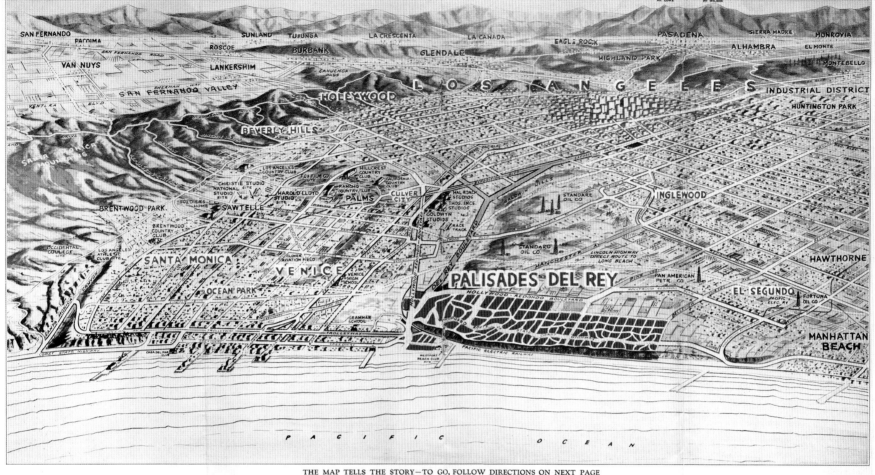

THE MAP TELLS THE STORY—TO GO, FOLLOW DIRECTIONS ON NEXT PAGE

Los Angeles' Most Accessible Beach
Boulevards, Major Highways Converging at Palisades Del Rey

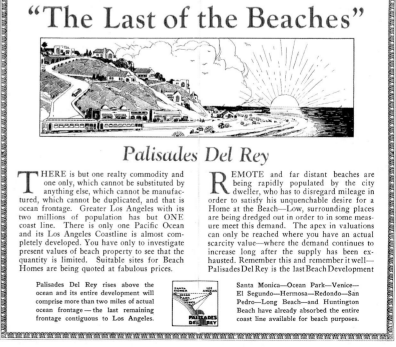

"The Last of the Beaches"

Palisades Del Rey

THERE is but one realty commodity and one only, which cannot be substituted by anything else, which cannot be manufactured, which cannot be duplicated, and that is ocean frontage. Greater Los Angeles with its two millions of population has but ONE coast line. There is only one Pacific Ocean and its Los Angeles Coastline is almost completely developed. You have only to investigate present values of beach property to see that the quantity is limited. Suitable sites for Beach Homes are being quoted at fabulous prices.

Palisades Del Rey rises above the ocean and its entire development will comprise more than two miles of actual ocean frontage — the last remaining frontage contiguous to Los Angeles.

REMOTE and far distant beaches are being rapidly populated by the city dweller, who has to disregard mileage in order to satisfy his unquenchable desire for a Home at the Beach—Low, surrounding places are being dredged out in order to in some measure meet this demand. The apex in valuations can only be reached where you have an actual scarcity value—where the demand continues to increase long after the supply has been exhausted. Remember this and remember it well—Palisades Del Rey is the last Beach Development

Santa Monica—Ocean Park—Venice—El Segundo—Hermosa—Redondo—San Pedro—Long Beach—and Huntington Beach have already absorbed the entire coast line available for beach purposes.

1915

Treasure Map NEWPORT BALBOA OCEAN and BAY

Treasure Map NEWPORT BALBOA OCEAN and BAY

1939   CSL

LOS ANGELES COUNTY SPORT LAND

LOS ANGELES SPORT

X OLYMPIAD LOS ANGELES 1932

1928   CSL

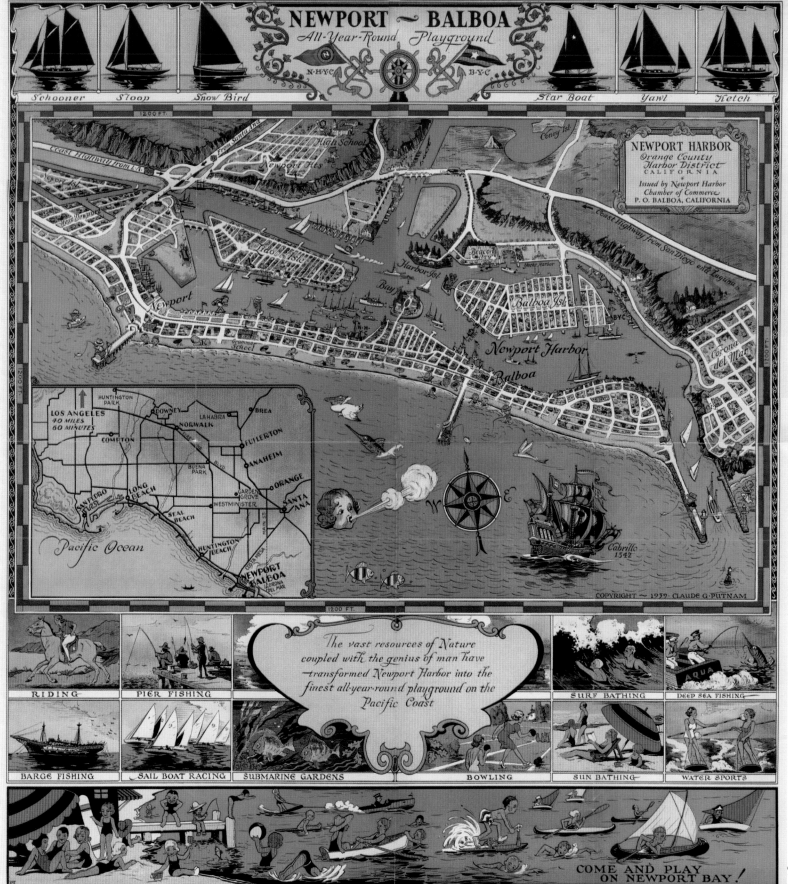

NEWPORT ~ BALBOA
All-Year-Round Playground

Schooner · Sloop · Snow Bird · Star Boat · Yawl · Ketch

NEWPORT HARBOR
Orange County
Harbor District
CALIFORNIA

Issued by Newport Harbor
Chamber of Commerce
P. O. BALBOA, CALIFORNIA

LOS ANGELES
40 MILES
60 MINUTES

Pacific Ocean

Cabrillo 1542

COPYRIGHT ~ 1939 CLAUDE G. PUTNAM

The vast resources of Nature coupled with the genius of man have transformed Newport Harbor into the finest all-year-round playground on the Pacific Coast

RIDING · PIER FISHING · SURF BATHING · DEEP SEA FISHING

BARGE FISHING · SAIL BOAT RACING · SUBMARINE GARDENS · BOWLING · SUN BATHING · WATER SPORTS

COME AND PLAY ON NEWPORT BAY!

97

1939   CSL

Hotel
Del Monte

Del Monte
California

CIRCA 1920 | CSL

Watering Places and Delightful Resorts: California for the Tourist

California is delightful at any season of the year — California in winter is ideal;
and the qualities that constitute its attraction for tourists and health
and pleasure-seekers are such as to call them back, year after year.

from *California, Winter's Summer Garden*, 1915

In thirty-five minutes, see her [Los Angeles'] *bejewelled ocean cincture, a galaxy of beach-towns that have the rich blue of the Pacific as an allurement every day in the year, and where surf bathing is indulged in every day, almost without exception. Santa Monica, Ocean Park, Venice, Playa del Rey, Manhattan, Hermosa, Redondo, San Pedro, Balboa and Newport are all reached directly with express electric cars direct from Los Angeles. Then, in the other direction stand the mountains with their Mt. Lowe Railway, Carnegie Observatory, and the cool and delicious canyons, where running brooks sing to sunshine-kissed trees, and gigantic mountain sides and cliffs keep putting on ever-changing garments of colour* (sic) *and tone for the delection of the elect.*

George Wharton James, 1914

Authors and artists enthusiastically exploited California's abundant natural wonders and man-made pleasures. Resort and hotel owners, as well as others who launched recreational ventures for the tourist and health seeker, also employed handsome brochures, pamphlets and postcards. California's relatively mild winters offered potential tourists welcome respite from mid-western and eastern blizzards and ice storms. California's equally touted temperate summers also provided escape from uncomfortable heat and humidity. Resort hotels and lodges equipped with swimming pools, golf courses, archery ranges, croquet lawns and other diversions catered to the well-to-do. Many resorts included spas and other health features for the invalid. As Norton P. Chipman, writing in 1904 for the California State Board of Trade publication, *California, The Land of Promise,* put it: *California is a universal sanitarium.*

Those who were serious about health could consult *California as a Health Resort*, published in 1916. Written by Dr. F.C.S. Sanders of Cambridge University, it was not only the quintessential guide to the state's mineral springs and health resorts, but also the most elegantly produced publication of its type. Among the favorite places of health seekers noted by Sanders was Richardson Mineral Springs located in the mountains of Butte County. With equal enthusiasm, a colorful 1930s era brochure, with the motto *Snap Back to Health!*, described this bucolic resort in great detail. Richardson Springs provided extensive facilities and acreage for rest, recuperation and recreation. The best exercise facilities, food, accommodations and free medical advice completed the package. The owners described the resort as *The Home of the Soft Shirt*, their reference to informal, unpretentious service.

Although substantial hotels were built in San Francisco and Sacramento in the 1850s and 1860s, the hey-day of grand hotels, resorts and spas came in the following decades with the expansion of railroads and touring companies who targeted the traveler seeking comfort, luxury, amusement and convalescence. Two elegant examples built in San Francisco during the 1870s included the Baldwin Hotel and the Palace Hotel. The urban hotel would continue to appeal to both the business traveler and the "upscale" family tourist in the decades to come.

Other fashionable destinations were more removed from urban centers. The Southern Pacific Company opened the lavish Del Monte Hotel on the Monterey Peninsula in 1880. To promote it and the Southern Pacific town of Pacific Grove, the railroad hired journalist Ben C. Truman to undertake a nation-

99

wide whistle-stop tour in the fall and winter of 1880. Armed with 25,000 pamphlets and 1,000 photographs of the hotel, he stumped the countryside extolling the railroad's entry into the hotel business.

A promotional brochure of 1915, encouraging motor travel south of San Francisco, highlighted *the extraordinary beauties of Monterey Bay and Del Monte, its world-famed resort.* The brochure's author continued: *Motoring through this region, around the "seventeen-mile drive" and its many extensions, is so perfect as to be almost unreal. The entire coast line southward is a success of watering places and delightful resorts, culminating in Santa Barbara.* The list of famous resorts extends to Riverside's The Mission Inn which began serving guests in the 1870s and to the elegant Del Coronado built near San Diego in 1888.

Raymond Excursions, a Boston-based touring company, provided refuge to weary easterners by opening one of the most popular of all California resorts, their own Raymond Hotel in Pasadena. The owners claimed that their clients were rescued from Boston snowstorms and delivered to the fragrant orange groves of balmy southern California. Again acknowledging the frequent tie-ins between transportation and hotel operations, the Raymond Excursion pamphlets promised that *the Santa Fe... passengers... landed directly at its doors.*

In the 1921 edition of *On Sunset Highways, A Book of Motor Rambles in California*, Thomas Murphy mentioned the Ambassador Hotel on Wilshire Boulevard, erected in 1920, as a glowing addition to the list of excellent hotels for the tourist. His list also included the Green, the Maryland, the Raymond and Huntington hotels, all located in the Pasadena area. Another famed hotel of the southland, the Alexandria, claimed in its own publicity to be *one of the principal centers from which the discriminating traveler may best explore the Wonderland of Southern California.* Not all travelers in southern California could afford the luxuries of such exclusive hotels. Some hotels like the Redondo Beach offered a two-tiered plan: luxury rooms in the main building for the well-heeled and more modest and remote accommodations for budget-conscious guests. By 1925, stated a Los Angeles Chamber of Commerce publication, travelers could also choose among twenty-six auto camps in the southern region.

A 1907 Southern Pacific publication, *California's Coast Country*, extolled the attributes of *The New Casino and Tent City of Santa Cruz*, a northern California coastal community. Reporting on the resort's ambitious plan to serve as a seaside haven and on the activities available to visitors, the brochure boasted: *The expenditures for the new Pavilion, the plunge baths, the electric light plant and the esplanade were over $500,000. Twenty thousand summer visitors can be comfortably accommodated at Santa Cruz...Here...is a center for sporting anglers after King Salmon, Barracuda and other game fish.*

Northern California's rugged natural wonders, once they could be reached by train or auto, attracted tourists to a variety of hotels, spas and camp grounds. In the 1870s, large summer vacation estates and lodges were built around Lake Tahoe. Intrepid travelers would ride by train to Truckee then transfer to stagecoach and, in later days, to the Tahoe Railway for the remainder of the trip. By 1915, highways extended to Lake Tahoe and Yosemite. Once state roadways were completed in the vicinity, motorists could travel from Sacramento to Tahoe in one day. With the advent of paved roads, other travel options included busses or motor coaches owned by companies such as the Pierce-Arrow Lines.

From the earliest days of tourism, unequaled hiking, fishing, swimming, gambling and exquisite scenery were the rewards of such a rigorous excursion. In addition to private homes and lodges, accommodations ranged from the simple cottages and tents of the Emerald Bay Camp and Hotel to the luxurious rooms of Tahoe Tavern with its nine-hole golf course, tennis courts and swimming plunge for summer, and its skating, skiing and toboggan rides in the winter.

Further south, Yosemite was certainly the highlight for adventurers of all backgrounds and interests. Beginning in the 1850s, this awe-inspiring area of "wonder and curiosity" beckoned artists, writers, naturalists and more adventurous tourists. Of the fifty-eight illustrations included in Charles Nordoff's famous 1872 publication, *California: A Book for Travellers and Settlers*, at least fifteen featured Yosemite. Edwin Markham, in his 1914 publication *California The Wonderful*, quoted ecstatic responses to this masterwork of nature from Ralph Waldo Emerson, Horace Greeley and Japanese-born poet Yone Noguchi. Even the often uncredited authors of promotional pamphlets were inspired to their most eloquent heights as the writer for a pamphlet on Camp Curry proved:

Dawns of saffron and flame from high mountain passes, moonrises where the silver light creeps slowly back from your feet until it pierces the deepest canyons between you and the jagged crest of the Sierra Nevada — from Benson Lake on the north,

100

where a cup of dusky red-gold holds the vivid blue of many a hundred summer skies to the gray and frozen austerity of Mount Lyell on the south, this park of yours is worth seeing.

Paintings and photographs of Yosemite by 19th century artists emphasized the panoramic grandeur of mountains and "big trees" in contrast to the diminutive position of humans and animals within this unique corner of the universe. However, such idyllic vistas could not remain forever removed from the general public. The first hotel in Yosemite was built in 1859. In 1864, by order of President Lincoln, Yosemite Valley was set aside as a state park. By 1890, the surrounding area became a national park, and in 1905, the federal boundaries extended to include Yosemite Valley and Mariposa Grove, an area of nearly 1,200 square miles. In later years, guide books and other promotional ephemera reflected increased human incursion in Yosemite: automobiles, for example, were shown emerging from tunnels carved through giant sequoia trees.

Early in the 20th century the Auto Club claimed a victory when Yosemite National Park was opened to motor travel. In time, autos far exceeded trains in transporting visitors into the Park. The Wawona Hotel, located above the valley floor, was opened in 1875 as part of Yosemite National Park. The elegant crisp white Victorian lodge perched on long, rolling green lawns provided its summer guests every possible comfort including this promise in its c. 1920 promotional literature: *there are no mosquitos at Wawona.* Motorists could also seek accommodations at the luxurious Hotel Ahwahnee, opened in 1927. Camp Curry, founded in 1899, provided more rustic yet comfortable accommodations in the form of *bungalows,* [which fit] *harmoniously into the forest background... tents, set in clusters among the trees, hedged about by dogwood and azalea and lilac in a succession of flowering loveliness...* [and] *central buildings, with their boulder-set fireplaces.*

The same Curry family who opened Camp Curry in Yosemite also ran the popular Lebec Lodge on the Ridge Route, a forty-eight-mile stretch between Los Angeles and Bakersfield. Operated under contract with the Automobile Club of Southern California and catering to the unique needs of the motorcar traveler, this establishment was an example of another California phenomenon— the *motel* — which proliferated along the ever expanding network of highways throughout the state.

It is not surprising that the photogenic wonders of Tahoe and Yosemite and the seductive charms of semi-tropical South-

ern California would lure visitors from all points of the globe. However, promoters also found ways to create tourist appeal for desert areas and to create such tourist meccas as Palm Springs. *Our Araby: Palm Springs and the Garden of the Sun,* written by J. Smeaton Chase and first published in 1920, offered a unique view of the geographical wonders of the area. It targeted as well, interests of the tourist and seasonal (winter and spring) resident. Chase, who also wrote *Desert Trails* in 1919, considered desert flora, *botanically speaking, a new world.* He prophesied emergence of a *Palm Springs School of Painters* and discussed the presence of the movie industry. As Chase pointed out, Palm Springs "stood in" for Algeria, Egypt, Palestine, Mexico, Australia, and India. The appearance of "film stars" was a great attraction. Tourists could enjoy expected amenities, horseback riding, "motoring," and — with the growing enthusiasm for aviation — "flying." The desert climate, he wrote, offered health benefits to those with lung, kidney and nerve ailments. Obviously written before the push for tourism and settlement, Chase's book encouraged appreciation for the natural features of the area, its serene qualities and its indigenous population. He mentioned the Desert Inn as providing the best accommodations with assurance of a "piped-water system." Train and postal service were taken for granted at the time. However, electric lights had not yet arrived and he seemed to take pleasure in the fact that Palm Springs was *free of the everlasting jingle of the telephone.* Chase's account stands in contrast to Palm Springs development in succeeding years. By the 1930s, tourism with a particular boost from the movie industry, grew enormously.

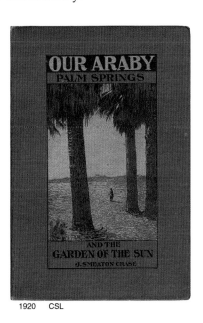

1920   CSL

101

"The Cedars of Lebanon," 17 Mile Drive

Restless Sea at Point Joe, 17 Mile Drive

Inspiration Point, Scenic Drive

Snow White Sand and Turquoise Sea

1920   CSL

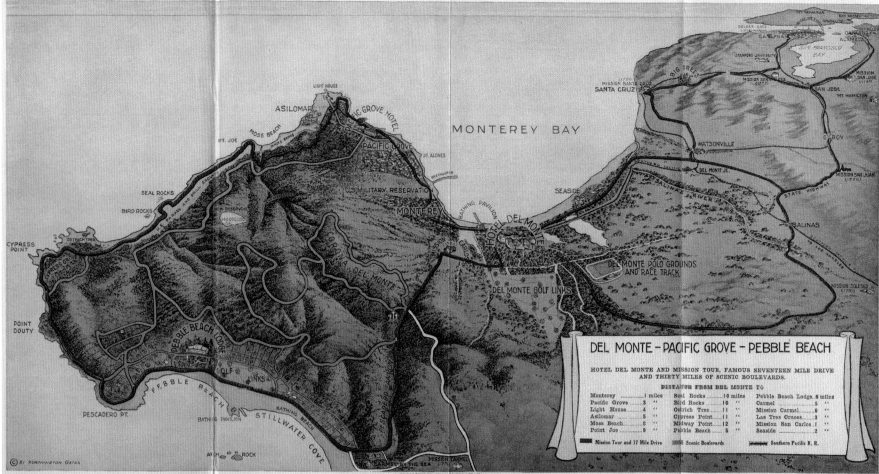

MONTEREY BAY

DEL MONTE – PACIFIC GROVE – PEBBLE BEACH

HOTEL DEL MONTE AND MISSION TOUR, FAMOUS SEVENTEEN MILE DRIVE
AND THIRTY MILES OF SCENIC BOULEVARDS.

DISTANCE FROM DEL MONTE TO

Monterey	1 miles	Seal Rocks	10 miles	Pebble Beach Lodge	6 miles
Pacific Grove	3 "	Bird Rocks	10 "	Carmel	5 "
Light House	4 "	Ostrich Tree	11 "	Mission Carmel	6 "
Asilomar	5 "	Cypress Point	11 "	Las Tres Cruces	3 "
Moss Beach	6 "	Midway Point	12 "	Mission San Carlos	1 "
Point Joe	9 "	Pebble Beach	5 "	Seaside	2 "

Mission Tour and 17 Mile Drive   Scenic Boulevards   Southern Pacific R. R.

CIRCA 1920   CSL

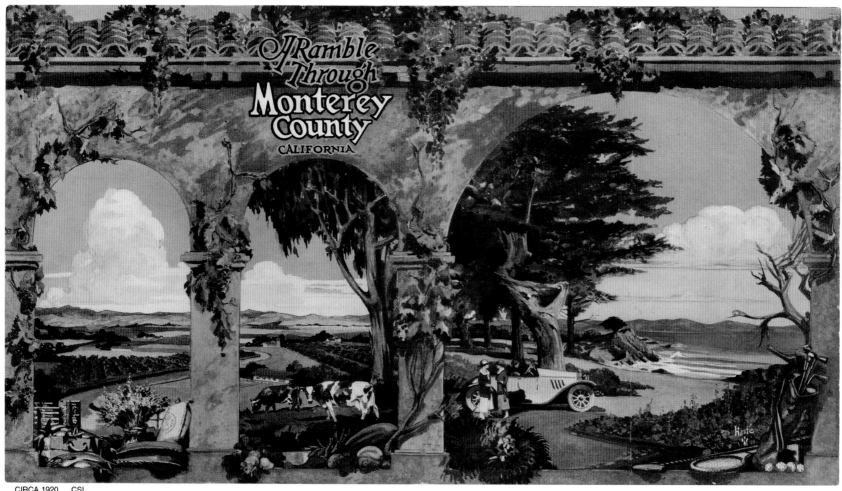

A Ramble Through Monterey County CALIFORNIA

CIRCA 1920   CSL

California DEL MONTE PACIFIC GROVE PEBBLE BEACH   California DEL MONTE PACIFIC GROVE PEBBLE BEACH

ON MONTEREY BAY   ON MONTEREY BAY

CIRCA 1920   CSL

THE LURE OF A LAND BY THE SEA

1922   CSL

103

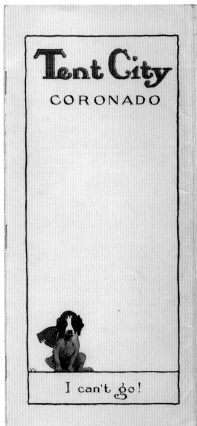

Tent City
CORONADO

I can't go!

Tent City
CORONADO

Let's go to Tent City!

RAILROAD RATES
Santa Fe Route.

Excursion fares to Coronado Tent City and return, in effect June 1st, and good returning September 30th, 1913.

Alessandro	$ 4.50	Lamanda Park	$ 4.50
Anaheim	3.50	Los Angeles	4.00
Arlington	4.25	Ludlow	12.00
Azusa	4.50	Mojave	10.00
Bakersfield	11.95	Monrovia	4.50
Barstow	9.35	Murrieta	5.00
Casa Blanca	4.25	Needles	16.00
Claremont	4.75	North Pomona	4.75
Colton	4.50	Oceanside	2.25
Corona	4.00	Olive	3.50
Cucamonga	4.75	Orange	3.50
Daggett	10.00	Oro Grande	6.95
Dinuba	15.70	Pasadena	4.25
East Highlands	4.75	Perris	4.75
Elsinore	5.00	Redlands	4.75
Escondido	2.75	Riverside	4.25
Fresno	16.05	San Bernardino	4.50
Fullerton	3.55	San Jacinto	5.00
Glendora	4.75	Santa Ana	3.50
Hanford	15.05	Stockton	20.85
Hemet	5.00	Temecula	5.50
Highland	4.75	Upland	4.75
Inglewood	4.25	Victorville	6.65
Johannesburg	10.00	Visalia	14.80
La Mirada	3.75	Winchester	5.00

Low fares from Arizona, New Mexico and other points to San Diego.

1913   CSL

CORONADO TENT CITY

OUR TENTH SEASON 1909

1909   CSL

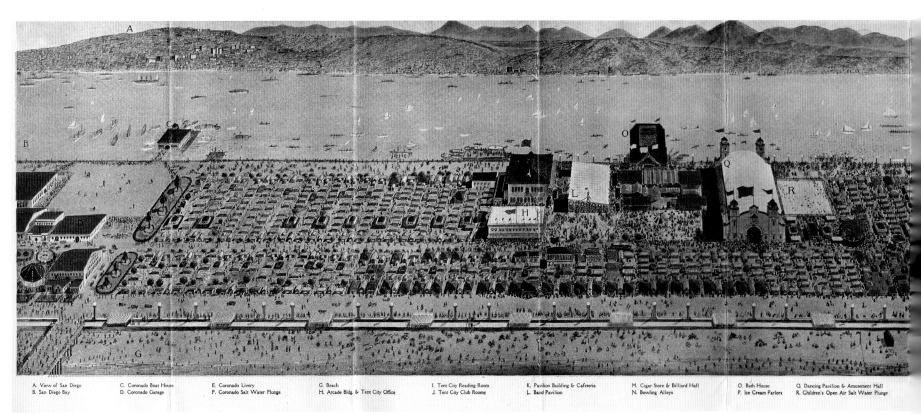

A. View of San Diego
B. San Diego Bay
C. Coronado Boat House
D. Coronado Garage
E. Coronado Livery
F. Coronado Salt Water Plunge
G. Beach
H. Arcade Bldg. & Tent City Office
I. Tent City Reading Room
J. Tent City Club Rooms
K. Pavilion Building & Cafeteria
L. Band Pavilion
M. Cigar Store & Billiard Hall
N. Bowling Alleys
O. Bath House
P. Ice Cream Parlors
Q. Dancing Pavilion & Amusement Hall
R. Children's Open Air Salt Water Plunge

1913   CSL

OUTDOORS AT
CORONADO

CSL

S. Merry-go-round in Children's Play Ground
T Children's Play Ground

WH BULL

1916

105

CSL

1936   CSL

CSL (from Paraiso Springs)

106

Hotel El Paso de Robles,
Paso Robles Hot Springs,
California.

CSL

BARTLETT SPRINGS

"HEALTH IN EVERY DROP"

LAKE COUNTY, CALIFORNIA

SAN FRANCISCO OFFICE: 71 BLUXOME STREET

CIRCA 1920s   CSL

SOVTHERN CALIFORNIA

THE HOTELS AND RESORTS
THAT HAVE MADE ITS FAME

1906   CSL

Hotel
Raymond
Pasadena,
"Crown
of the
Valley"

CSL

Riverside, California, set amid orange groves,
is a paradise on earth where life is luxury
every day in the year.   Its chief hotel

THE NEW GLENWOOD

FRANK A. MILLER   PROPRIETOR

is a marvel of comfort, with equipment and surroundings artistic, picturesque and satisfying
WHY NOT GO THERE?
For details write to Frank A. Miller, The Glenwood,
or the Secretary Chamber of Commerce

RIVERSIDE CALIFORNIA

IN WRITING TO ADVERTISERS PLEASE MENTION SUNSET

1903

Hotel
Wentworth
Pasadena

CSL

CSL

CSL

Hotel Arcadia, Santa Monica, Cal.

—W.H.F.—1157

CSL

109

HOTEL
S.T FRANCIS
On Union Square
SAN FRANCISCO
CALIFORNIA
One of the World's Great Hotels
THOS. J. COLEMAN
MANAGER.

110

CSL

SAN FRANCISCO
The PALACE HOTEL

Management of
Halsey E. Manwaring

CSL

FAIRMONT HOTEL

SAN FRANCISCO
CALIFORNIA

D. M. LINNARD
LESSEE
LE ROY LINNARD
MANAGER

CSL

MAY 1929   10 CENTS
SUNSET

Lane Publishing Company ~ San Francisco

Yosemite National Park

Southern Pacific

CSL

IN SPRING

IN SUMMER

1926   CSL

YOSEMITE ROAD GUIDE

CAMP CURRY

1922   CSL

112

YOSEMITE
CALIFORNIA'S ALL-YEAR PLAYLAND

YOSEMITE
CALIFORNIA'S ALL-YEAR PLAYLAND

IN AUTUMN

IN WINTER

1925

Yosemite

MAURICE LOGAN

SOUTHERN PACIFIC

1922   CSL

CSL

1915

1915

114

1916   CSL

1925

STANDARD OIL
BULLETIN

PUBLISHED BY THE STANDARD OIL COMPANY OF CALIFORNIA
JUNE   1929

115

STANDARD OIL
BUL·L·ETIN

PUBLISHED MONTHLY BY THE STANDARD OIL COMPANY (CALIFORNIA)
MAY 1920

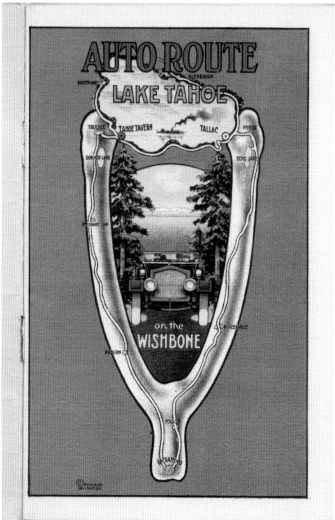

AUTO ROUTE
LAKE TAHOE
on the
WISHBONE

CSL

TAHOE TAVERN
LAKE TAHOE
California

CSL

Globin's LAKE TAHOE   Globin's LAKE TAHOE

AL TAHOE   AL TAHOE
FRANK GLOBIN Owner-Manager   FRANK GLOBIN Owner-Manager

1924   CSL

TAHOE TAVERN

LAKE TAHOE, CALIFORNIA

CSL

117

Catalina ISLAND CALIFORNIA

FLYING FISH

COPYRIGHT MCMLI BY CURT TEICH & CO., INC., CHICAGO, U.S.A.

Tent City, Catalina Island.

Just a few of many Jim

12509

1909

SANTA CATALINA ISLAND California "THE MAGIC ISLE"

POSTAGE 1½¢ WITHOUT MESSAGE

COPYRIGHT 1939 BY CURT TEICH & CO., INC., CHICAGO, U.S.A.

1939

Souvenir Folder of CATALINA ISLAND, CALIFORNIA

Published by Western Publishing & Novelty Co., Los Angeles.

© C. T. & Co.

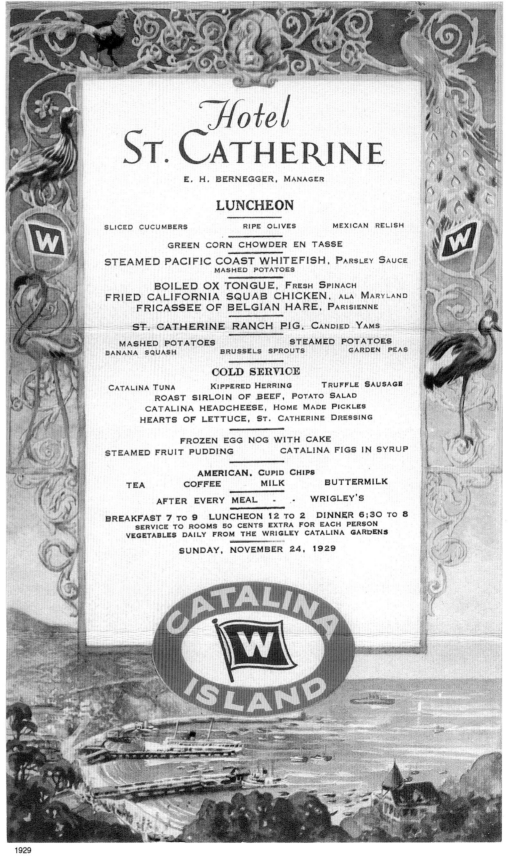

Hotel ST. CATHERINE

E. H. BERNEGGER, MANAGER

LUNCHEON

SLICED CUCUMBERS   RIPE OLIVES   MEXICAN RELISH

GREEN CORN CHOWDER EN TASSE

STEAMED PACIFIC COAST WHITEFISH, PARSLEY SAUCE
MASHED POTATOES

BOILED OX TONGUE, FRESH SPINACH
FRIED CALIFORNIA SQUAB CHICKEN, ALA MARYLAND
FRICASSEE OF BELGIAN HARE, PARISIENNE

ST. CATHERINE RANCH PIG, CANDIED YAMS

MASHED POTATOES   STEAMED POTATOES
BANANA SQUASH   BRUSSELS SPROUTS   GARDEN PEAS

COLD SERVICE

CATALINA TUNA   KIPPERED HERRING   TRUFFLE SAUSAGE
ROAST SIRLOIN OF BEEF, POTATO SALAD
CATALINA HEADCHEESE, HOME MADE PICKLES
HEARTS OF LETTUCE, ST. CATHERINE DRESSING

FROZEN EGG NOG WITH CAKE
STEAMED FRUIT PUDDING   CATALINA FIGS IN SYRUP

AMERICAN, CUPID CHIPS
TEA   COFFEE   MILK   BUTTERMILK

AFTER EVERY MEAL - - WRIGLEY'S

BREAKFAST 7 TO 9   LUNCHEON 12 TO 2   DINNER 6;30 TO 8
SERVICE TO ROOMS 50 CENTS EXTRA FOR EACH PERSON
VEGETABLES DAILY FROM THE WRIGLEY CATALINA GARDENS

SUNDAY, NOVEMBER 24, 1929

CATALINA ISLAND

1929

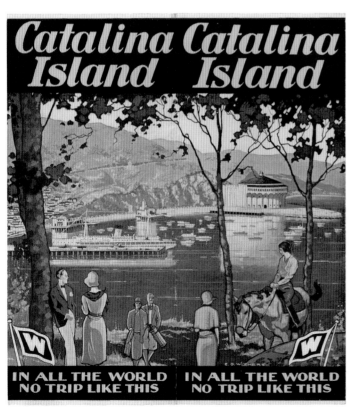

Catalina Island   Catalina Island

IN ALL THE WORLD NO TRIP LIKE THIS   IN ALL THE WORLD NO TRIP LIKE THIS

1931   CSL

119

Motor Land

MAY · 1927

120

1920s   CSL

Through and Above California: Motor Rambles and the Aviation Age

We climbed many mountains, visited the endless beaches, stopped at the famous hotels, and did not miss a single one of the twenty or more old Spanish missions. We saw the orange groves and palms of Riverside and Redlands, the great oaks of Paso Robles, the queer old cypresses of Monterey, the Torrey Pines of La Jolla, the lemon groves of San Diego, the vast wheat fields of the San Joaquin and Salinas Valleys, the cherry orchards of San Mateo, the great vineyards of the Napa and Santa Rosa Valleys, the lonely beauty of Clear Lake Valley, the blossoming desert of Imperial, and a thousand other things that make California an enchanted land. And the upshot of it all was that we fell in love with the Golden State — so much in love with it that what I set down may be tinged with prejudice; but what story of California is free from this amiable defect?

Thomas Murphy, 1915

In his book, *On Sunset Highways*, Thomas Murphy drew upon his experiences of motoring through California for three consecutive years. The title page identified Murphy as a member of the Automobile Club and undoubtedly he undertook the trip with the Club's sponsorship. His travels each year during April and May focused on Santa Barbara southward although he took at least one extended trip to San Francisco. He explained that April and May were the best months for motor travel because roads were less dusty and the hills more green. One could not reach Yosemite or Tahoe by automobile during the spring months, he explained. At that time of year the tourist relied upon trains. Murphy's beautifully illustrated book extolled the virtues of motor travel and, of course, the scenery from his window.

During this time period, train travel, especially with sleeping accommodations, to such spots as Yosemite and Tahoe, was considered too expensive for average travelers. Automobiles, on the other hand, offered a more affordable alternative. As road ways were built, they provided even more access between urban and rural destinations.

121

CSL

At this writing the two trunk lines from San Diego to San Francisco are practically completed and the motorist between these points, whether on coast or inland route, may pursue the even tenor of his way over the smooth, dustless, asphalted surface at whatever speed he may consider prudent, though the limit of thirty-five miles now allowed in the open country under certain restrictions leaves little excuse for excessive speeding. It is not uncommon to make the trip over the inland route, about six hundred and fifty miles, in three days, while a day longer should be allowed for the coast run.

In 1921, Murphy produced a revised edition of his book

with a post-war update on road development. His writings exemplify the role of the automobile in early 20th century life and its prominence in both the imagery and language of promotional material. While the motorcar was seen by the public as a democratizing influence by expanding travel opportunities, many brochures and pamphlets continued to portray motoring as more of an affluent activity and, therefore, a symbol of wealth. In brochures, elegant touring machines filled with carefree pleasure-seekers made their way through plein-air landscapes of dappled light and verdant, rolling hills. However, closer inspection of the text often revealed useful information for the traveler of any means: mileage, maps,

122

VISIT STUDEBAKER AT THE AUTO SHOW—FEB. 20-28—(See Page 10)

CSL

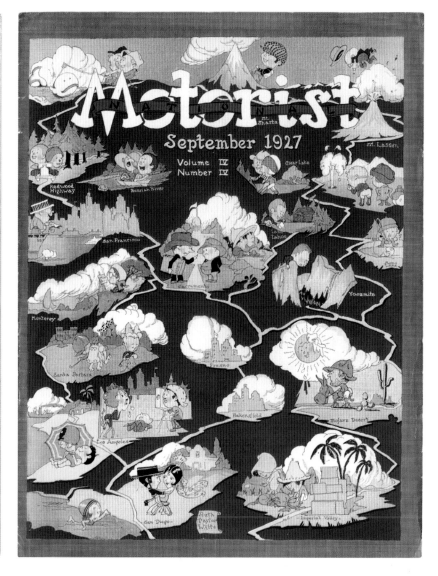

obstacles, lodging, landmarks, and local attractions. Text and image incorporated at least two symbols of California gold: constant golden sunshine and the black gold of petroleum. A 1925 Los Angeles Chamber of Commerce publication boasted: *Southern California offers the best developed highway system on the continent... California leads all states... in its provision of improvement and extension of its roads.*

After World War I, several publications reflected growing enthusiasm for aviation. Flying, once restricted to military purposes and sport, was becoming a common method of travel. Designs for almost all aviation related promotional literature were characterized by a machine-age aesthetic, most with

elegant Art Deco motifs. Promotional pamphlets and travel guides also increased the use of "aerial" views to show featured locations. Harris M. Hanshue, President of Transcontinental and Western Air, Inc., writing in 1931, recommended that *every person from the East or Middle West coming to California for the first time should make the initial trip, at least, by airplane.* As evidence that aviation for pleasure or commerce was an industry, certain hotels and other businesses began to cater exclusively to the air traveler. Hotel Oakland, for example, promoted itself as *The Crossroads of the Air* and as the *Pacific Coast Aviation Headquarters.* Anticipating travelers' needs for this *new method of rapid transportation* was seen as progressive management.

123

W·H·BULL

1915

CALIFORNIA TOURS

SAN FRANCISCO

HOTEL PLAZA
Post and Stockton Streets
SAN FRANCISCO'S NEWEST HOTEL
In the center of business and amusement!
A high class tourist Hotel, famous for its Cuisine, Comfort and Service
Automobile touring information gladly furnished on request
Stockton and Sutter Garage One Block From Hotel

Rates:
European plan, - $1.50 per day up
American plan, - $3.50 per day up
Management of C. A. Gonder

COMPLIMENTS of the
NORTHERN CALIFORNIA HOTEL ASSOCIATION

CALIFORNIA TOURS

COMPLIMENTS of the
NORTHERN CALIFORNIA HOTEL ASSOCIATION

1917   CSL

Touring Tips to Tourists

Sight Seeing in Southern California
via Harry L. Weisbaum's
GOLDEN STATE AUTO TOURS

Harry L. Weisbaum's

Golden State Auto Tours are personally conducted and are the best organized Auto Sight Seeing Trips in Southern California. We use high-grade pneumatic tired cars exclusively. Our trips are carefully arranged, avoiding all repetition and so routed that you visit the many out-of-the-way beauty spots along the way, which adds greatly to your pleasure and are seen in no other way. We conduct eight separate and distinct trips. Reservation for all Golden State Auto Tours can be made at the following places in Los Angeles. Be sure and make your reservations a day or two in advance for the one- and two-day trips.

Alexandria Hotel Auto Desk, 5th and Spring Sts.
Ask Mr. Foster, anywhere in the United States.
American Express Co. Travel Division 719 So. Blvd.
American Travel Bureau, 517 So. Spring St.
Baltimore Hotel Tourist Agent, 5th and Los Angeles.
Clark Hotel, Cigar Stand, 426 So. Hill.
Cook's Tours (Thos. Cook & Sons), 515 So. Spring St.
First National Bank, Long Beach, Calif.
Hotel Chandler, 834 So. Main St.
Hotel Savoy, Cigar Stand, 601 W. 6th St.
Huntington Hotel, Hotel Clerk, 752 So. Main.
New Broadway Hotel, 205 No. Broadway
Peck Judah Co., Tourist Agents, 623 So. Spring St.
H. G. Stevens Co., Inc., Owl Drug Store, 6th and Bdwy.
Stowell Hotel Auto Desk, 416 So. Spring St.
The Poinsettia Information Bureau, 445 So. Hill St.
Trinity Hotel, Cigar Stand, 847 So. Grand.
Van Nuys Hotel Auto Desk, 105 W. 4th St.
Westminster Hotel, Hotel Clerk, 4th and Main.
Women's Hotel, 639 So. Grand.

We operate 26 cars, all built for comfort, consisting of Whites, Kings and Packards. Insist upon riding with the Golden State Auto Tours while in Los Angeles.
SMITH-BARNES CORP., LOS ANGELES

Sight Seeing Trips
Every Hour—On the Hour
STARTING FROM THE
HOTEL ROSSLYN
455 South Main Street, Corner Fifth
14246-60911-Main 9246-Ask for GOLDEN STATE
SEEING
LOS ANGELES   PASADENA   THE BEACHES
RIVERSIDE and REDLANDS   SAN DIEGO
CATALINA ISLAND   TOPANGO CANYON
and the TRIANGLE TRIP

1921   CSL

124

LOS ANGELES NEW HOTEL ROSSLYN AND ANNEX

RATES PER DAY (European Plan)

	Single	Double
50 Rooms without Bath	$1.50	$2.00
150 Rooms without Bath	2.00	$2.50 - 3.00
300 Rooms, Private Toilet	$2.00 - 3.00	3.00 - 4.00
575 Rooms, Private Bath	2.50 - 4.00	3.50 - 6.00
25 Corner Suites, $7.00 and $8.00		

A MAGNIFICENT, safe, double-deck Bus provides transportation to and from the various railroad stations. The Rosslyn is the only hotel in Los Angeles supplying this service free of charge to guests.

The Rosslyn Hotel and Annex are very conveniently located to all business, shopping and amusement districts. Headquarters for one of the largest Sight-seeing Auto Touring Companies of the Pacific Coast. Also, one block away is the Pacific Electric Station, which operates large, safe, steel cars to most of the beaches and to beautiful surrounding country and famous mountain resorts, golf clubs, etc.

CSL

1921   CSL

1922   CSL

125

CIRCA 1930 CSL

CIRCA 1933 CSL

1930 CSL

1924 CSL

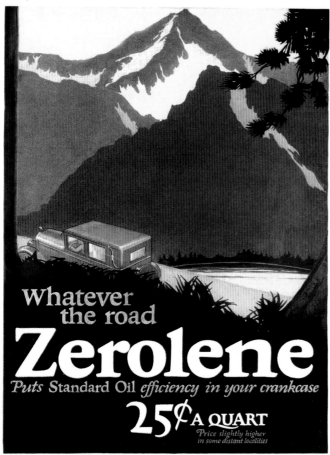

Whatever
the road
Zerolene
Puts Standard Oil *efficiency in your crankcase*
25¢ A QUART
*Price slightly higher
in some distant localities*

1927

The Charm of California Life.

Is experienced in its fullness and at its best when motoring over California's perfect highways in the luxurious cars furnished by an automobile service that has become noted the country over. The Tanner Service, owning over one hundred high-class cars, supplies every motoring want. Write, wire or telephone us at either of the cities named and be relieved of your motoring details.

Tanner Automobile Service

*Authorized and Approved
by these Hotels*   Pasadena   Santa Barbara   San Francisco   *The Same Perfect Service in Each City*

1920   CSL

SEE CALIFORNIA THE OLDEN
on your "Roads to Romance"

FOLLOW the highway of the Mission Bells, though many of those bells are cracked and silent. El Camino Real, from San Diego to Sonoma, is peopled with the colorful ghosts of Spanish padres, gay caballeros and dark-eyed senoritas.

Nearly a score of missions are still standing. On the low wall of a well-spring a senorita plays her guitar, though the well has been dry these many years and the senorita sleeps under an olive tree. Caballeros with jingling spurs and seven-gallon hats come riding by. Reverend fathers in cowl and cassock pass and repass under the arches.

Thus you will live in the California of a century ago.

So speed in your car out of the present into the romantic past. Follow Jack and Ethyl, the honeymooning Motormates. They tell you every Wednesday night, of new places to go and sights to see.

All along the way, Associated dealers are waiting to give you detailed travel and resort information. Stop at the red, green and cream stations. Fill up with Associated Gasoline and your car will readily answer your urge to be going. Know the surge of its eager power, its quick acceleration, and its ability to give you long mileage.

Associated Oil Company
*Refiners of Associated Gasoline
Associated Ethyl Gasoline and
West Coast Motor Oil*

ASSOCIATED GASOLINE

*Wednesdays at 9 p.m.
—follow Jack and Ethyl
on "Roads to Romance"
over the Pacific Coast
Network of the National
Broadcasting Company*

Stations:
KOMO Seattle
KGW Portland
KGO Oakland
KPO San Francisco
KFI Los Angeles

1928

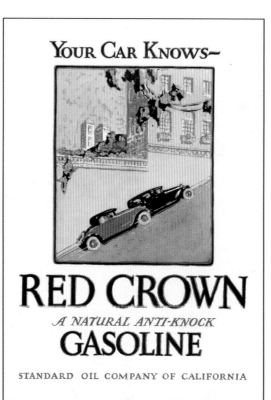

YOUR CAR KNOWS—

RED CROWN
A NATURAL ANTI-KNOCK
GASOLINE

STANDARD OIL COMPANY OF CALIFORNIA

1927

128

1926

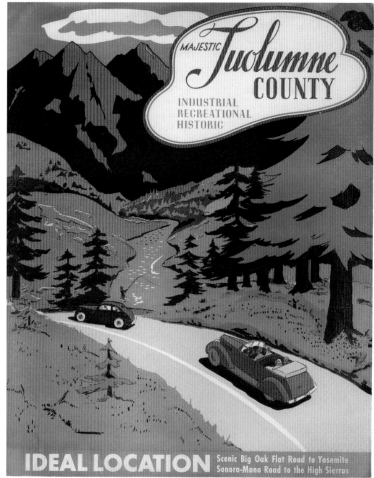

1940 CSL

1935 CSL

CSL

129

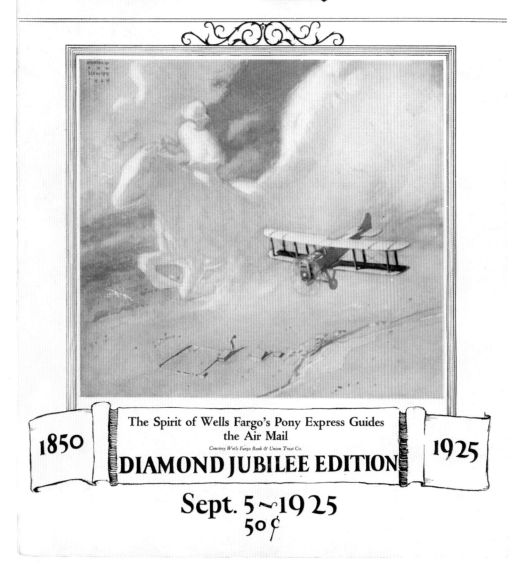

SAN FRANCISCO
News Letter

The Spirit of Wells Fargo's Pony Express Guides
the Air Mail

Courtesy Wells Fargo Bank & Union Trust Co.

1850   **DIAMOND JUBILEE EDITION**   1925

Sept. 5 ~ 1925
50¢

130

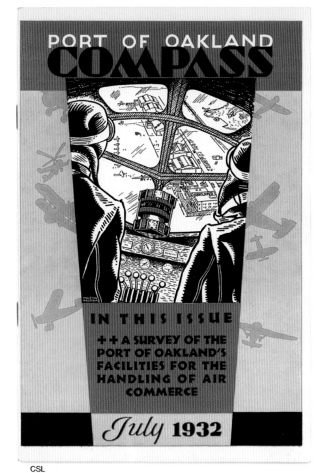

PORT OF OAKLAND
COMPASS

IN THIS ISSUE
+ + A SURVEY OF THE
PORT OF OAKLAND'S
FACILITIES FOR THE
HANDLING OF AIR
COMMERCE

July 1932

CSL

. . . . man-made birds
unsurpassed air service
. . the endless chain of
. . . . . . transportation

1931   CSL

AIR TRAVEL GUIDE
OAKLAND AND EAST BAY EDITION

TABLE OF CONTENTS

1929   CSL

MADDUX MADDUX
AIR LINES AIR LINES
DEPENDABLE DEPENDABLE

California..Mexico   California..Mexico
and the   and the
Southwest   Southwest

CIRCA 1930

KERN KERN
COUNTY COUNTY
AIRPORT AIRPORT

CIRCA 1930   CSL

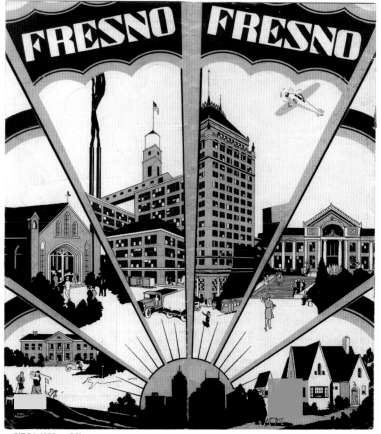

FRESNO FRESNO

CIRCA 1930   CSL

131

CALIFORNIA
IN 1915

RAYMOND & WHITCOMB CO.

Landmarks, Pageants and World's Fairs

Ho for California, the ever summer-land, with its skies of blue and gold, its green valleys and purple hills, emerald seas and sapphire lakes, desert sands and blooming meadows, giant forests and flowering orchards, red-woods and palm trees, violet vineyards and golden groves, its inns and missions, Indians and Movie Actors, Boosters and Buckaroos, Padres and Forty-niners, Spanish Dancers and Conquistadores — Land of exotic Beauty and glamorous Romance!

The Raymond-Whitcomb Tours to California, 1915

Hotels, resorts and auto-camps were not the only destinations available to tourists. Neither were the ocean beaches, deserts or mountains the only draw for the recreation-minded traveler. California's own "history" and the places — real or mythical — associated with past events created a new form of vacation pilgrimages.

Helen Hunt Jackson's novel, *Ramona,* published in 1884, and other efforts to recreate California's mythological romantic past, stimulated public interest in restoring the old Mission properties and recapturing the "Days of the Dons." Yet another tourist industry blossomed as a result of this Ramona mania in the form of travel books, plays and pageants. Mrs. A.S.C. Forbes, well known for writing on the days of the Missions and Spanish arcadia, was connected with the Department of History for the Women's Federation of Clubs. As a lecturer, she tirelessly campaigned on behalf of landmark preservation. In her 1903 book, *California Mission Landmarks and How to Get There,* she provided information on transportation, accommodations, rates, and distances from San Francisco and Los Angeles. Her guide book pointed to the need for additional funds to continue work begun on restoration of San Juan Capistrano, San Diego and San Fernando missions. She also showcased the arts and crafts of regional Indian groups in a section entitled *Other Sites and Treasures.* As evidence of the intended purpose of her booklet, she included two railway advertisements: *18 of the 21 Missions in California are reached <u>exclusively</u> by the Southern Pacific;*

and *the Sea Shore Resorts are best reached by the Salt Lake Route (Santa Fe Railway).*

Another who did much to promote the Mission era was John Steven McGroarty, author, poet, historian, U.S. Congressman and editorial writer for the *Los Angeles Times.* He is best remembered for creating *The Mission Play,* a popular, romanticized pageant of the missions from their founding to their demise and ruin. First produced in 1912, the play was held for many years at Mission San Gabriel. McGroarty's remarkable achievement interwove drama, music, poetry and painting. Colorful printed programs designed for each production were, in themselves, promotional brochures for California.

Parades, fiestas and fairs honoring holidays, local events, heroic deeds, technological advances and the abundant products of counties and, later, the state, took place from California's earliest days. While many celebrations were transplanted from *back home,* thereby reminding new settlers of fond memories and old roots, other celebrations such as the state's admission day and regional agricultural advances marked the pride in emerging, new communities. The author of an 1885 San Gabriel Valley Citrus Fair report capsulized this sentiment by stating that the purpose of their fair was to demonstrate *horticultural progress in* [the] *comparatively new industry of this valley.* The annual citrus exhibition inaugurated in Riverside in 1879, was soon credited for attracting *attention from abroad.* Organizers felt confident that the *success of the exhibitions*

133

proportionately makes the growth of the place. M. M. Estee, addressing a December 1886 Citrus Fair audience in Sacramento, also acknowledged the role of citrus fairs in attracting tourists and settlers. However, he went on to declare, *We need no boom that will bring millionaires; they are made here and need not be imported.*

California's early boosters knew that a major annual event, besides being entertaining, could bring ongoing attention to the region and work in tandem with other organized promotional efforts to attract tourists and home buyers. The Valley Hunt Club of Pasadena met in 1889 to develop an event for New Year's Day which could incorporate both traditional and currently popular sports with prizes offered to winning contestants. In addition, the ladies of the Hunt Club would crown winners with roses. An article announcing these plans appeared in the *Pasadena Star-News* on December 18, 1889: *the "Tournament of Roses" is a name well adapted to convey to the blizzard-bound sons and daughters of the East, one of the sources of enjoyment which, of the land of perennial sunshine, boast.* Citizens were invited to bring baskets of roses to the festival. Only local citizens knew that it rained the day the article appeared. However, it did not rain the day of the first Tournament of Roses, January 1, 1890. Two hundred and fifty people attended and the event was considered a great success. The Valley Hunt Club continued as an annual sponsor through New Year's Day, 1895, at which time the Pasadena Board of Trade appointed a committee to manage the event. In 1897, the Tournament of Roses Association formed giving institutional status to this increasingly popular event. The first football game associated with the Rose Parade came in 1902, but the contest did not become a regular feature until 1926. The Women's Division, also added in 1926, developed themes for the annual floral event.

The *Pasadena Star* and later, the *Pasadena Star-News and Post* published colorful annual programs with attractive covers and photographs of the "float" displays and lists of entrants. These publications included articles on Pasadena that presented the considerable assets of *The Ideal Home City* for the benefit of potential home seekers. As the 1931 edition of the Tournament of Roses Program explained: *Commercialism is... banned and as a result the great pageant assumes a unique place in this age of intensive advertising.* However, the annual printed programs served in effect as promotional literature.

Not all fairs were devoted exclusively to agriculture, horticulture and their by-products. Many incorporated wide-ranging exhibits of hand-made and machine-made products as well. Several fairs of the late 19th century celebrated the arrival of electricity for both commercial and residential use. In addition to local and state-wide fairs, California and her assets were also well represented at such world's fairs as Chicago's Columbia Exposition in 1893 and the 1904 St. Louis fair.

August 14, 1914, marked completion of the Panama Canal, one of the greatest engineering feats of the new century, and marked California's entry in the international economic arena. In 1915 and 1916, San Francisco and San Diego each hosted a world's fair to call attention to the canal and their cities. On the same day that San Diego, first U.S. port of call north of the Canal, announced that it would host an exposition, the San Francisco Chamber of Commerce made the same announcement for its city and port. Thus, the two cities were pitted as rivals for the honor and attention. Eventually they resolved the conflict: Two expositions were held. The Panama-California Exposition opened on December 31, 1914, in San Diego. An extended San Diego Exposition ran, under re-organized management, through 1916 and closed on January 1, 1917. The San Francisco fair, called the Panama Pacific International Exposition (P.P.I.E.), opened on February 20, 1915, and closed on December 4 that year. The railroads, who stood to benefit from increased tourism, developed packaged excursions to the west coast that included both fairs at no extra charge.

San Diego recreated its "romantic" past in scenic Balboa Park with Spanish "Colonial" style buildings designed by Bertram Goodhue. San Francisco projected its pride through majestic buildings erected on land fill at the northern edge of the city. The P.P.I.E. inspired a raft of promotional booklets. Each county of the state took pride in the celebrations, and most publications in the period carried the seal of the Panama Pacific Promotion Committee. A 1912 booklet published by the Sacramento Chamber of Commerce not only extolled its own many laudable features to the reader, but also tied its future to the P.P.I.E.:

The Panama Pacific International Exposition in 1915, is now but three years away, a fair which will startle the whole world with its magnificence and grandeur. The people of Sacramento only desire to develop their untold resources, build better and prettier homes, and beautify their city in every possible way and in this manner help prepare for that notable occasion... California is a great State, and as time rolls, the beautiful California of to-day will be but a pleasing recollection of the California of tomorrow.

134

SAN FRANCISCO'S STORY TOLD AND PICTURED By SAN FRANCISCANS

SUNSET

JUNE - JULY · 1906

10 CENTS A COPY
ONE DOLLAR A YEAR

NEW YORK: 349 Broadway
CHICAGO: 120 Jackson Blvd.
LONDON: 49 Leadenhall St.

SAN FRANCISCO
CALIFORNIA

CSL

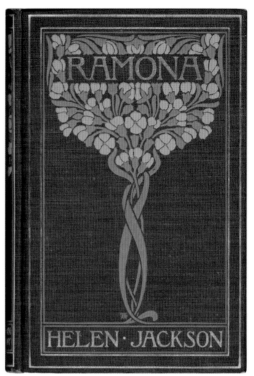

RAMONA

HELEN · JACKSON

1900

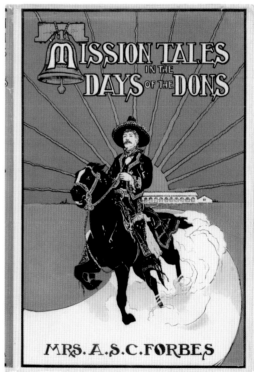

MISSION TALES IN THE DAYS OF THE DONS

MRS. A. S. C. FORBES

1926

135

PORTOLA FESTIVAL 1909 SAN FRANCISCO OCTOBER 19 TO 23

CSL

N. S. G. W. OFFICIAL POSTAL

ADMISSION DAY FESTIVAL 1910

SAN FRANCISCO · SEPT · 8 · 9 · 10

CSL

136

ADMISSION DAY 1910 FESTIVAL
SAN FRANCISCO
SEPTEMBER 8·9·10

CSL

ADMISSION·DAY·1910·FESTIVAL·
SAN FRANCISCO·
SEPTEMBER 8·9·10·

CSL

1915

ATLANTIC OCEAN

PANAMA CANAL from an Aeroplane

PACIFIC OCEAN   PANAMA

COPYRIGHT 1913 BY THE PANAMA-PACIFIC INTERNATIONAL EXPOSITION CO.

INFORMATION for Visitors to the PANAMA-PACIFIC INTERNATIONAL EXPOSITION San Francisco 1915

1c. Paid
San Francisco, Cal.
Permit No. 304

CSL (above and below)

133

PANAMA PACIFIC INTERNATIONAL · EXPOSITION · SAN FRANCISCO · 1915

EVERY NIGHT IS 4TH OF JULY AT THE EXPOSITION

1915

California's Best AUTO TRIP

1916

TO THE SAN DIEGO EXPOSITION "IT'S A BEAR"

CSL

NEW INTERNATIONAL EXPOSITION

NOW OPEN CLOSING DAY DEC. 31—

1916 San Diego California Exposition

Open All The Year 1916

A NEW International Exposition

CSL

140

1916

1916

-again during 1916

San Diego Exposition

Larger, more beautiful, more interesting than ever. Graced by the best and most elaborate foreign Exhibits which were at the San Francisco Exposition.

Reached by the Santa Fe All the way

Illustrated Booklets of trains and trip to California on request—
Jno. J. Byrne, Asst. Passenger Traffic Mgr. A. T. & S. F. Ry.
907 Kerckhoff Building, Los Angeles

141

CALIFORNIA'S MIDWINTER GREATEST EVENT

Third

National Orange Show

REDUCED RATES ON ALL RAILROADS

Feb. 17-22 1913

San Bernardino California

WESTERN LITHO Co. LOS ANGELES CAL.

CSL

San Bernardino California and Its Environments

1902   CSL

SECOND NATIONAL ORANGE SHOW
FIRST BIG EVENT 1912
FEB. 19 TO 24 1912
SAN BERNARDINO CALIFORNIA
REDUCED RATES ON ALL RAILROADS
OLSEN LITHO. CO. L.A. & S.F.

CSL

SIXTH NATIONAL ORANGE SHOW
California's MIDWINTER
Greatest EVENT
February 17-24-1916
San Bernardino California
WESTERN LITHOGRAPH CO. LOS ANGELES, CAL.

CSL

EIGHTH NATIONAL ORANGE SHOW
SAN BERNARDINO California
FEBRUARY 20 TO 28, 1918.
EXCURSION RATES ON ALL RAILROADS
"CALIFORNIA'S GREATEST MIDWINTER EVENT"
WESTERN LITHOGRAPH CO. LOS ANGELES, CAL.

CSL

THE MISSION PLAY

SECOND SEASON

SAN GABRIEL MISSION
NEAR LOS ANGELES CAL,

1912   CSL

BELL TOWER
OLD SAN GABRIEL MISSION

The
MISSION PLAY
by JOHN STEVEN McGROARTY
PRESENTED IN THE
MISSION PLAY HOUSE
AT OLD SAN GABRIEL MISSION
CALIFORNIA

1923-1924

Free Souvenir Programme/
NATIONAL CHAMPIONSHIP
SPEEDWAY RACES
LOS ANGELES CALIF.
Los Angeles Speedway Association
APRIL 10, 1921.

144

1921   CSL

CAUSEWAY CELEBRATION

SACRAMENTO, MAY, 11-14, 1916

EDW. M. MUSE

DESIGNED, ENGRAVED AND PRINTED IN SACRAMENTO

CSL

CSL

CSL

CSL

146

PASADENA STAR-NEWS TOURNAMENT NUMBER

1920

TOURNAMENT OF ROSES
PASADENA, CALIFORNIA

Frank E. Brown

CSL

147

MAKE YOUR MIND UP TO WIND UP IN
SUNNY CALIFORNIA

WORDS and MUSIC by FRED HOWARD & NAT VINCENT

Morse M. Preeman
Los Angeles, Calif.

1930

OUT IN CALIFORNIA

Music by
Homer Tourjée

Lyric by
Alfred Dalton

1921

CALIFORNIA STATE LIBRARY

In San Diego

WORDS and MUSIC
THOMAS H. SEXTON

Compliments of the SAN DIEGO-CALIFORNIA CLUB
CHAMBER OF COMMERCE BUILDING, SAN DIEGO, CALIFORNIA
"In San Diego, Where Life Means Most"

1921

148

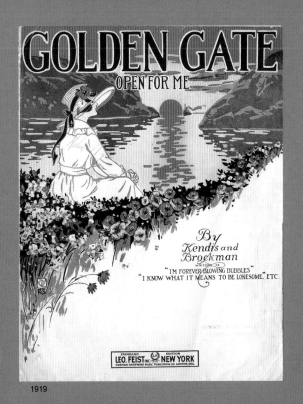

1919

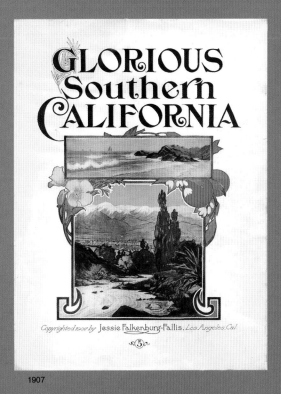

1907

1924

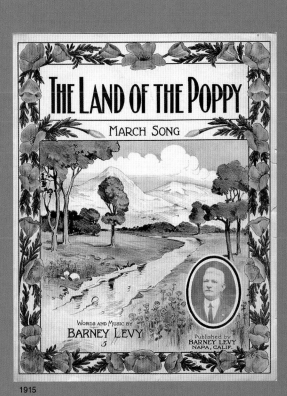

1915

SHEET MUSIC, COURTESY CSL

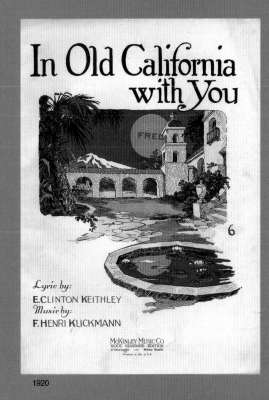

1920

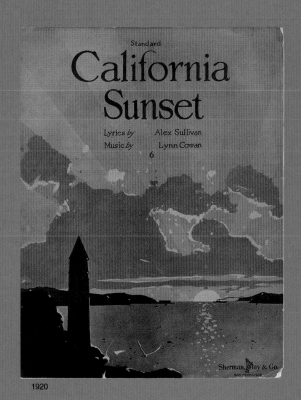

1920

149

APR 26 1935

AMERICA'S EXPOSITION

1935

CALIFORNIA
PACIFIC INTERNATIONAL
EXPOSITION
Opens in San Diego · May 29, 1935

CSL

Official Program
GOLDEN GATE BRIDGE
FIESTA
SAN FRANCISCO
MAY 27 - - - - - JUNE 2
1937

25¢

CSL

150

Coming Out of the Depression

John Steinbeck's literary masterwork, *The Grapes of Wrath*, published in 1939, portrayed the epic experience of the decade through the lives of the fictional Joad family and their odyssey to California. The Joads, struggling to survive along with many other migrant workers, discovered farms in the hands of big business and scant opportunity for work. Dorothea Lange's classic photograph, *Migrant Mother*, exuded the dignity of a mother in hopeless conditions, surrounded by her children. Both projected archetypal images of California and the Great Depression. Much of the promotional material of the period, however, did not present this picture to the world. Brochure illustrations portrayed sturdy laborers busily at work in fields or factories, their faces glowing with optimism. Most of these publications showed Californians entertained by their world's fairs and enthralled with structural feats such as the Golden Gate Bridge, accomplishments meant to boost the economy and to distract the weary. The brochures described communities with balanced growth, healthy industries and strong schools.

Several times during the 1930s, California took center stage in world events. In 1932, Los Angeles hosted the 10th Olympiad, and in 1935, San Diego presented another great Exposition in Balboa Park. Two years later, San Francisco celebrated completion of the Golden Gate Bridge with a remarkable Fiesta, and in 1939, California invited the world to celebrate its newest engineering wonder, the Oakland-San Francisco Bay Bridge. This celebration — called the Golden Gate International Exposition — was the last world's fair to take place before the United States entered World War II. Also known as the Treasure Island Fair because of its location on the man-made island link between the two expanses of the Bay Bridge, it took place from February 18 to December 2, 1939. (This exposition opened earlier and closed later than the World's Fair in New York.)

Celebrating San Francisco's position among the countries of the Pacific Rim, it evoked the architecture and cultures of Central and South America as well as Asia. A Treasure Island brochure published by the Southern Pacific stated:

The railroads of the United States, Canada and Mexico invite you to see the West and the San Francisco World's Fair... we promise you an experience you'll remember all your life. Your destination will be the Golden Gate International Exposition on San Francisco Bay, but en route you'll see the West, too... Rail fares to the San Francisco World's Fair are very reasonable. We invite you to compare them with the cost of other forms of transportation, remembering always the advantages of speed, safety and comfort of rail travel.

Once again, hundreds of thousands of people, from all points of the compass, heeded the call to California and the lure of *golden dreams*. This Fair did not disappoint. However, as with previous expositions, the enchanting buildings and attractions erected for the celebration were not meant to last. Eugen Neuhaus, a noted art historian commented:

After it has run its relatively brief course, the site so magically created and transformed will be cleared to become an aviation field of the Federal Government... We should make every effort to accomplish some lasting results in applying the inspiring lessons of the Exposition to the permanent improvement of our cities and in the West generally.

Reflecting a significant change in the state's and country's priorities, the magical site did transform into a major military installation. Did inspiring lessons from the World's Fair prevail as Neuhaus and others hoped? This *Land of Eden* survived the ravages of a strained economy during the 1930s by putting its best face forward. The next call to California would come, not because of California's health-giving climate and golden dreams, but because of a war that changed the world.

151

CALIFORNIA OLYMPIC YEAR ROAD MAP

STANDARD OIL PRODUCTS

STANDARD STATIONS, INC.
RED WHITE & BLUE DEALERS

STANDARD OIL COMPANY OF CALIFORNIA

CSL

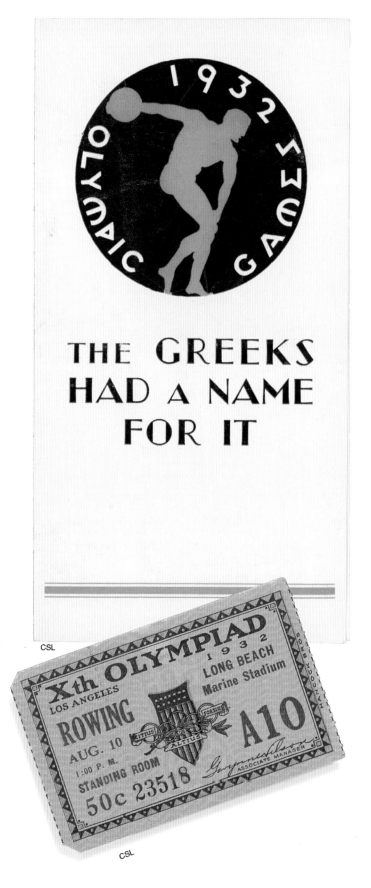

1932 OLYMPIC GAMES

THE GREEKS HAD A NAME FOR IT

CSL

Xth OLYMPIAD
LOS ANGELES
1932
LONG BEACH
Marine Stadium
ROWING
AUG. 10
1:00 P. M.
STANDING ROOM
A10
50c 23518
ASSOCIATE MANAGER

CSL

152
CSL

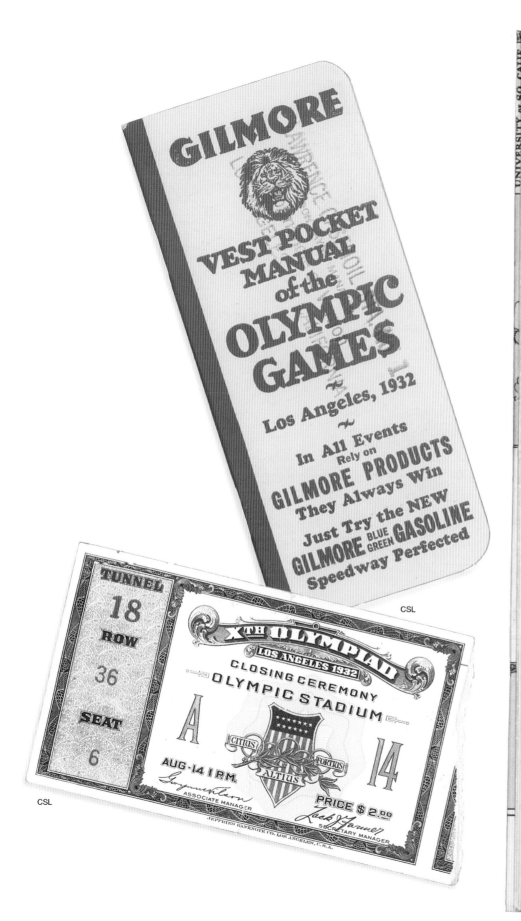

GILMORE

VEST POCKET MANUAL of the OLYMPIC GAMES

Los Angeles, 1932

In All Events
Rely on
GILMORE PRODUCTS
They Always Win

Just Try the NEW
GILMORE BLUE GREEN GASOLINE
Speedway Perfected

CSL

TUNNEL
18
ROW
36
SEAT
6

XTH OLYMPIAD
LOS ANGELES 1932
CLOSING CEREMONY
OLYMPIC STADIUM

A

CITIUS FORTIUS
ALTIUS

AUG. 14 1 P.M.

Gwynne Wilson
ASSOCIATE MANAGER

PRICE $2.00

Zack J. Farmer
SECRETARY MANAGER

14

JEFFRIES BANKNOTE CO. LOS ANGELES, U.S.A.

CSL

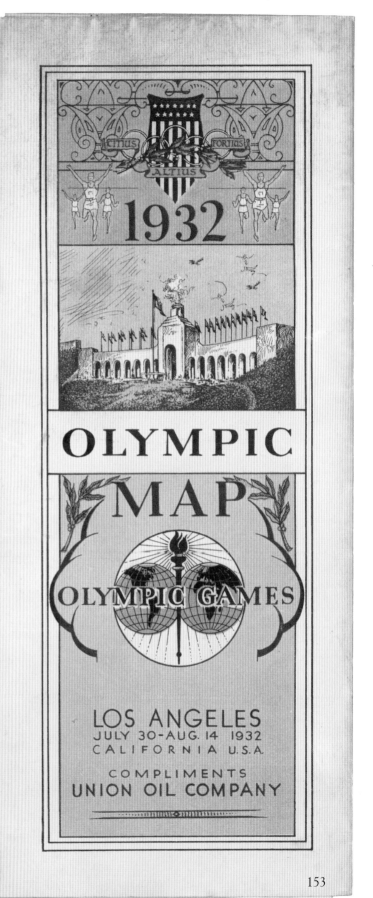

1932

OLYMPIC

MAP

OLYMPIC GAMES

LOS ANGELES
JULY 30-AUG. 14 1932
CALIFORNIA U.S.A.

COMPLIMENTS
UNION OIL COMPANY

153

CSL

STANDARD OIL
BULLETIN

PUBLISHED BY THE STANDARD OIL COMPANY OF CALIFORNIA
APRIL   1932

CSL

STANDARD OIL
BULLETIN

PUBLISHED BY THE STANDARD OIL COMPANY OF CALIFORNIA
JANUARY   1934

1939-1940   CSL

1931

PICTORIAL
SAN DIEGO
CALIFORNIA

1931   CSL

155

TREASURE ISLAND
SAN FRANCISCO WORLD'S FAIR

In the Pacific Basin area, you'll thrill to the romance of the Orient

Facing the Federal Building, the Towers of the East beckon to adventure

156   1939   CSL   (above and right)

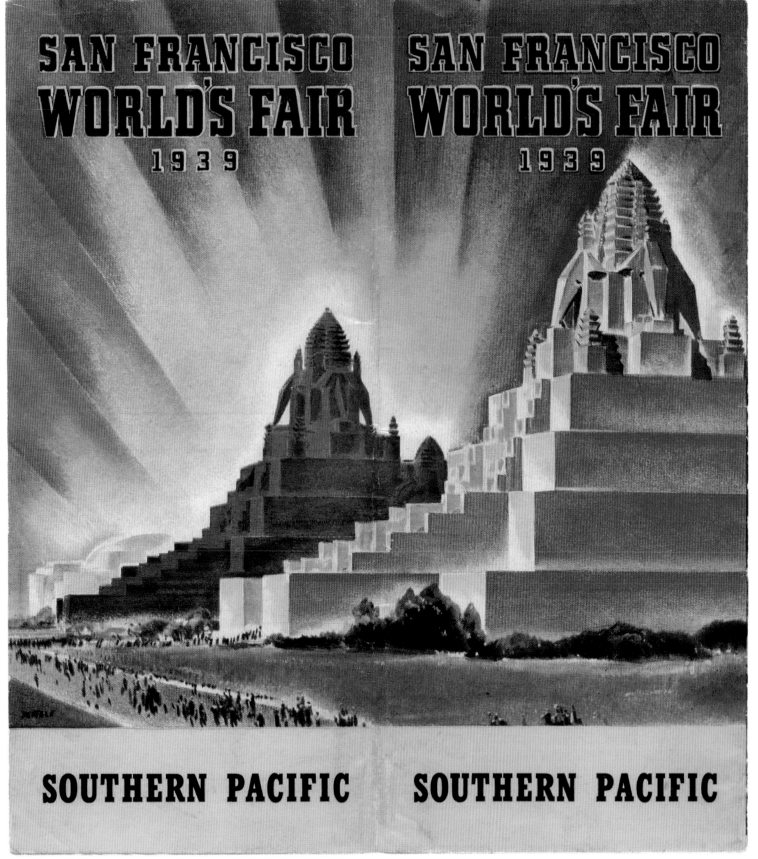

SAN FRANCISCO WORLD'S FAIR 1939

SAN FRANCISCO WORLD'S FAIR 1939

SOUTHERN PACIFIC

SOUTHERN PACIFIC

1939   CSL

157

Epilogue

California Calls You represents a thirty-year love affair with California promotional literature. While working at the Henry E. Huntington Library, I was introduced by Dr. Edwin Carpenter to the joy of ephemera and the delights of boomer publications. Since then, the visual power of the brochures, postcards, posters, and labels instilled in me a passion for the subject and converted me into a "Californiac." Moreover, the florid language of the booster, particularly that of Major Ben Truman, only whetted my appetite for this sub field of Californiana. In my mind, there is no greater joy than rummaging through a box or file drawer of ephemera and pulling out one of those beautifully illustrated city or county brochures. They represented what California hoped to be— that elusive Eden of health, wealth, and happiness.

The places of my employment, Huntington Library, California Historical Society, and California State Library all possess wonderful collections of booster material. Immediate access to them served to increase my appreciation for the artists, writers, and organizations who produced this paean to California. Opportunities to display these brochures and reproduce them as illustrations for books and articles brought me into contact with knowledgeable collectors. Antiquarian bookstores, rare book and ephemera fairs, and flea markets proved to be rich hunting grounds for these colorful publications. Bringing back to my institution an armload of new additions was most satisfying.

Promotional brochures and booklets are now coveted as much as rare books and manuscripts, and reflecting their desirability, libraries with significant California collections are now formally cataloging them rather than tossing them into a box or stuffing them into a file cabinet. Their importance in understanding the development of California cannot be overlooked.

In many respects this book is an outgrowth of an exhibition of promotional literature which I organized for the California State Library at an antiquarian book fair in San Francisco. Linda and Wayne Bonnett of the Windgate Press expressed to me their appreciation and enthusiasm for the visual power of the exhibition. This started us on our way to producing a book that would put in one place the best as well as a representative sampling of California "boosteriana." My wife KD, a thorough researcher and art educator, joined in this endeavor. She quickly became enraptured by not only the imagery but also by the booster organizers and writers and their relentless campaign to bring people to the Golden State. For both of us, *California Calls You* is the culmination of a long cherished goal.

This visual essay would not have been possible without the enormous resources of the California History Section of the California State Library in Sacramento. For generations this institution has systematically collected and organized promotional literature. We are also in debt to the many dealers and collectors who brought additional examples to our attention including Ken Harrison, Robert Hawley, Wendell Hammon, Ron Lerch, Argus Books, and Dawson's Book Shop. The late Herb Caplan was always an inspiration. We are most grateful to the Windgate Press for realizing the potential of this book and for creating such an elegant and arresting design.

GFK

CALIFORNIA CALLS YOU

UNION PACIFIC

Appendices and Notes

ABOUT THE ARTISTS:

Commercial artists working from 1870 to 1940 experienced considerable changes and improvements in the way graphics were printed. As printing technology improved, full-color illustrations and photographs in brochures became possible, fanciful hand lettering and oil paintings could be reproduced. For the artist working against a deadline at the mercy of an impatient art director, the new technology was a blessing that also opened new possibilities. Bold colors and designs, subtle shadings and fine lines became tools readily incorporated into the artist's technique.

From the earliest California promotional booklets and posters, artists developed a symbolic shorthand to express ideas and myths about California: the poppy, the orange, the color gold, the palm tree, and the redwood tree. These symbols appear repeatedly in California promotional publications and, although they became hackneyed through repetition, they were effective in quickly conveying a message. The mission ruins, a crumbing arch, particularly combined with a modern backdrop, suggested California's rich past and promising future. The solitary padre, to a lesser extent, suggested the same thing. Various depictions of fruit represented California's fertility, a grizzly bear its wildlife. Scenes combining in close proximity snow-capped mountains, orange groves, oil wells, and happy families became common. Despite the obvious nature of these devices, they worked. One can easily imagine the appeal of such sun-soaked scenes to a winter-bound Midwestern farmer.

Following are examples of how skilled commercial artists of the period created variation using ordinary graphic symbols.

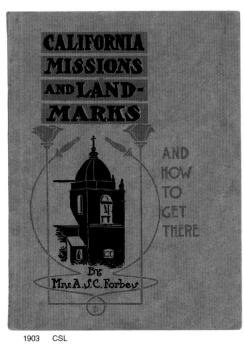

1903   CSL

CIRCA 1930   CSL

1903   CSL

160

1894 CSL

1924 CSL

CIRCA 1930 CSL

1905 CSL

161

1908   CSL

Copa de Oro
The State Flower.

CALIFORNIA
HER
RESOURCES AND POSSIBILITIES

FOURTEENTH ANNUAL REPORT
OF THE
CALIFORNIA STATE BOARD OF TRADE
For the Year 1903.

BY
N. P. CHIPMAN, PRESIDENT.
Chairman of the Committee on Industrial Resources.

Submitted March 8, 1904.

PUBLISHED BY THE
CALIFORNIA STATE BOARD OF TRADE
OFFICE AND EXHIBITION HALL
Union Ferry Building. : : San Francisco, Cal.

1904   CSL

1912   CSL

1916

162

Motor Land

JULY · 1929   20c THE COPY

CSL

BEAR IN MIND *Sacramento* CALIFORNIA 1929

CSL

CALIFORNIA REPUBLIC

N·S·G·W·

LOS ANGELES, SEPT. 9TH 1897

1897   CSL

GOLDEN STATE HIGHWAY

CSL

163

Artists' Biographies

*Yes, California is quite as beautiful as her poets insist
and her painters prove.*
Inez Haynes Irwin
The Californiacs, 1916

The following short biographies are meant to introduce the reader to the lives and careers of many commercial artists and designers whose work is found in this publication. As will readily be seen, little is known about a number of them. In some cases, names are identified on cover designs or text illustrations but little or no information surfaced in standard biographical sources, Artists Files, and California City Directories (listed in the Bibliography). Further, many of the illustrations reproduced in this volume were created by uncredited artists. Page numbers are given for examples of artists' work.

John Arthur Bazart (1889-1971)

Although Bazart's name can be found on several covers for the *Tournament of Roses* programs, little is known about his career. He was born in New York, and known to be living and working in the Los Angeles area by 1915. His name, sometimes identified as a portrait artist, appears in Los Angeles Directories of the 1930s. *Page 146, top right, bottom right.*

Arthur E. Beaumont (1890-1978)

Beaumont, born in England, emigrated to California via Canada by 1910. Initially he worked on cattle ranches in central California, but eventually, he moved to San Francisco where he studied art at the Mark Hopkins Institute. He pursued his artistic training at U.C. Berkeley, the Los Angeles School of Art and Design, and in England and France. He was working as a commercial artist in the early 1920s, and from 1927 to 1928, taught commercial art at Chouinard Art Institute in Los Angeles. During this period he produced artwork for several promotional brochures. A member of the U.S. Naval Reserve in the early 1930s, he produced maritime scenes and portraits in watercolor. He spent the remainder of his life in southern California teaching privately, and producing artwork for magazines and promotional brochures. *Page 50, bottom right; 89 bottom left.*

Frederick John Behre (1863-1942)

Behre, born in San Francisco, was associated with Bancroft as an artist/designer for a number of years. Most sources indicate that he lived in southern California from 1888 forward. Known to live in Pasadena for some of that time, he was both a painter and photoengraver. *Page 163, bottom left.*

Oscar W. Bergesen (1892-1984)

Bergesen was born in Illinois and attended Northwestern University. In 1917, he moved to Pasadena with the U.S. Army Engineers. Following this service, he moved to San Francisco and apprenticed with the McCann Advertising Agency while pursuing studies at the California School of Fine Arts. By 1925, he had returned to Los Angeles where he continued to support himself with commercial art work. During the mid-1940s, he relocated to Chicago where he continued his career. In 1976, he returned to California to be with his family. *Page 50, top left; 126, top and bottom left; back flap (Fresno).*

Adriano (dates unknown) and Augusto (1879-1968) Bissiri / Bissiri Studio

Brothers Adriano and Augusto Bissiri emigrated from Sardinia, and by 1915, opened a commercial art studio in Los Angeles. Augusto was known as a fine artist while most Directories identified Adriano as a commercial artist. However, it is Augusto's name which appears on the cover of the 1926 issue of *California Motoring.* Adriano, who specialized in lettering, worked for Western Lithograph from the 1920s to 1950s. He was known for designing titles for motion pictures. *Page 123, left.*

Carl Oscar Borg (1879-1947)

Borg, who achieved success as a painter, etcher and illustrator, was born in Sweden. Initially he worked as a seaman, but at age 20, took the opportunity to work as apprentice to a portrait and marine painter in London. From there he emigrated to New York City in 1901. Two years later he moved to California, eventually making his way to Los Angeles where he studied with William Wendt. He came to the attention of Phoebe Apperson Hearst through whose patronage he pursued further art study in Paris and Rome. Upon returning to California, he taught at the Art Institute in Los Angeles from 1918 to 1924. He then moved to Santa Barbara where he taught at the School of Arts. Between 1924 and 1935, he traveled between San Francisco, Los Angeles and the Grand Canyon producing vivid images of western life and scenery for which he gained his reputation. His portrayals of the Hopi, Navajo, cowboys, missions and western landscapes found their way into his paintings and illustrations.. He was active in many art clubs and earned numerous awards, among them, the Gold Medal at the 1904 St. Louis Exposition, the Silver Medal at the Panama-Pacific International Exposition, and Silver and Gold Medals at the Panama-California Exposition in San Diego. He was detained in Sweden during the war years but returned to Santa Barbara where he died in 1947. *Page 11, top right.*

Randal William Borough (1878-1951)

Born in Tennessee, Borough emigrated at some point to San Francisco where he lived until at least 1911. From there he moved to Los Angeles where he remained for a few years. He then moved east and became known for his portraits. *Page 30 left, page 69 center, 136 left.*

Frank E. Brown

Brown designed the covers for several *Tournament of Roses* programs and lived in Pasadena. Local Directories listed him variously as an artist, as selling art goods, and by 1935, as selling pictures and frames. *Page 146 bottom left, 147.*

William H. Bull (1861-1940)

A prolific and successful commercial artist, Bull was born in Buffalo, New York. In recalling his impetus for moving to California, he once stated: *In 1893, I wandered out to Chicago and the California exhibit of fields and mountains at the world's fair sent me out here.* Settling first in Fresno, he then spent a year living and painting in the Sierra region. In 1902, along with Gottardo Piazoni, Xavier Martinez and others, Bull co-founded the California Society of Artists. His career as a commercial artist accelerated from that point, leading to commissions for magazine covers and other work.

Southern Pacific Company hired Bull as their first commercial artist and by 1915, he also produced work regularly for *Sunset Magazine*. He lived primarily in San Mateo and produced illustrations for chamber of commerce publications. Bull succeeded as both a commercial artist and fine artist, producing striking landscape paintings of California. *Page 22, 25, 27 top left, 29, 36 left, 69 left, 72 right, 73 top left, 86 top, 103 bottom right, 105 right, 112 left, 114 right, 139 top right, 158.*

Arthur James Cahill (1878-1970)

Cahill, who enjoyed success as a painter and illustrator, was born in San Francisco. He studied art at the San Francisco School of Design and in Paris. In the early 1890s, he produced illustrations for the *San Francisco Chronicle*, the *San Francisco Examiner*, and the *San Francisco Call*. After the 1906 earthquake and fire, he headed to New York where he worked for the *New York World, Saturday Evening Post, Harpers, Colliers,* and others for the next four years. Returning to San Francisco, he worked for *Sunset Magazine*, first as staff artist, then as art editor. He also produced work for other Southern Pacific publications. Following this period, he achieved great success as a portraitist of such notables as Gov. James Rolph, Jr., Gen. John Pershing and President Herbert Hoover. At some point, he moved to southern California as indicated by listings in Pasadena and Los Angeles Directories from the late 1920s to mid-1930s. He then moved to Texas before returning to live in California. Throughout his career, he was active in art circles as a member of the Bohemian Club, the San Francisco Art Association and the Los Angeles Art Association. *Page 11, 24 top right.*

Gerald Cassidy (1879-1934)

Cassidy worked as a commercial artist in Los Angeles from about 1913 to the early 1920s. Born in Ohio, he is better known as a Santa Fe artist. In Cincinnati, he studied under the well-known painter Frank Duveneck. Cassidy studied also at the National Academy of Design and Art Students League in New York where he began his art career. He was drawn west initially because of his interest in Native Americans and the desert landscape. By 1912, Cassidy was living and working in Santa Fe producing images of New Mexico Indians for the tourist trade. He moved to California and, after living in Los Angeles for nearly 10 years, returned to Santa Fe where he achieved fame through murals and portraits. *Page 63, bottom left.*

Merle T. Cox

Cox achieved success as a commercial artist in Inglewood where he worked from the mid-1920s through the 1930s. He lived the latter part of his life in San Francisco. *Page 89, top left.*

Wesley Raymond DeLappe (1887-1952)

Born in Maxwell, California, DeLappe worked for the McCann-Erickson Advertising Agency (known earlier as H.K. McCann Co.), in San Francisco, for 50 years. In addition to his commercial art career, DeLappe was also known as a painter and etcher. *Page 33 right, 37 center, 116 left, 119 left, 120 left.*

John Frank Derby (1875-1943)

Derby was born in Plymouth, Pennsylvania and moved with his family to Los Angeles at a young age. As a teenager, he studied at the Art

Students League. By the turn of the century, he was designing posters and labels for the Los Angeles and Union Lithograph companies, and eventually, he became chief of design for Western Lithograph where he worked for twenty years. He was also a member of the Painters and Sculptors Club of Los Angeles. Although he gained widespread recognition for his commercial work, he was also an accomplished composer of semi-classical, romantic music. *Page 75, 143 bottom left and bottom right.*

(Lafayette) Maynard Dixon (1875-1946)

Dixon's fascination with western subject matter came from growing up on a ranch near Fresno, and from the stories he heard as a young boy. In 1891, his family moved to Coronado, near San Diego. About this time, he sent a letter to artist Frederick Remington whose encouragement inspired Dixon to become an illustrator. Two years later he enrolled in the Mark Hopkins Art Institute but remained for only three months. That same year, Dixon's first illustration appeared in the *Overland Monthly*. In the next few years, he established himself as an illustrator at the *San Francisco Morning Call*, and earned commissions for prestigious magazines and for books by leading authors. By 1899, he was hired as art director for the *San Francisco Examiner Sunday Magazine*, where he remained for less than a year. In 1900, he undertook his first sketching trip through the southwest and two years later he began his first work for *Sunset Magazine*. Unfortunately the earthquake and fire of 1906 destroyed his San Francisco studio and most of his early work. He continued working as an illustrator, but in 1907, he accepted his first mural commission from the Southern Pacific Company. Shortly after that, he moved to New York and continued his commercial assignments. By 1912, he returned to San Francisco and expanded his interests to fine art. He won a bronze medal for art at the Panama Pacific International Exposition in 1915. In 1916, he started work for the commercial firm, Foster and Kleiser. He was extremely active during the 1920s and 1930s, completing major mural commissions and taking part in exhibitions throughout the country. Although he continued to accept occasional commercial art commissions, he primarily produced murals and paintings in the next decades. In 1940, Dixon and his third wife, Edith Hamlin, moved to Utah where they established a studio and began work on a home in Arizona. They moved between these two homes for the rest of his life. *Page 135 left, 154 left and right.*

Constance Farris

Farris produced illustrations for southern California publications at the turn of the century, such as *California & Sketches of the Southwest*, published by the *Los Angeles Times-Mirror* in 1901, and promotional brochures for the San Bernardino Board of Trade. *Page 142, right.*

Joe Duncan Gleason (1881-1959)

Born in Watsonville, Gleason grew up in Los Angeles. His artistic talent was recognized early and by age 14, he was working for the Union Engraving Company. He received his first art training at the University of Southern California, and continued at the Mark Hopkins Institute after moving to San Francisco in 1899. At the same time, he took a job at the Sunset Engraving Company. He pursued further art education in Chicago and New York. While in New York, he also accepted commercial art commissions. In subsequent years, he traveled to Mexico and Europe, then returned to Los Angeles in 1914, where he worked for Young and McAllister, producing commercial work while also taking up his interest in easel painting. He exhibited widely, earned a gold medal at the California-Panama Exposition in San Diego in 1915, and enjoyed membership in several southern California art organizations. He also worked for the art departments of MGM and Warner Brothers movie studios. *Page 40 top right, 41.*

Porter M. Griffith (1889-1969)

Griffith was born in Tennessee. He settled in San Francisco in 1907 where he worked as a commercial artist through the 1940s. For some of that time, he maintained an office/studio in the Hearst Building. He spent his later years in Sausalito. *Page 148, top right.*

George W. Hall

Little information exists on the artist who designed the striking cover for the Los Angeles County *Sportland*, published in 1928. His name appears in the 1922 Los Angeles Directory, and his listing indicates that he was employed by the Western Lithograph Co. *Page 96, bottom left.*

Homer A. Hamer (1883-1967)

Hamer, born in Ohio, settled in Los Angeles by at least 1910. However, he lived for a short period in San Diego and is listed in the 1915 San Diego Directory as an artist for the Pacific Photo Engraving Company. By the early 1920s, Hamer was again working as an artist in Los Angeles. *Page 148, bottom right.*

Sam Hyde Harris (1889-1977)

At age 15, Harris emigrated with his family from his native England to Los Angeles. By age 21, he was already a prolific freelance commercial artist, doing *everything from show cards to wall work*, by his own account. He studied art at the Art Students League of Los Angeles, and from 1913 to 1917, traveled in Europe. The 1922 Los Angeles Directory identified Harris as a designer of "Art Posters." In 1925, he taught painting at Chouinard Art Institute, indicating his continued interest in both commercial and fine art. His commercial art commissions came from Southern Pacific, Union Pacific and Santa Fe Railroad Companies, to name a few. He is remembered for the windmill logo which he designed for Van de Camp's Bakeries. His paintings, which built on the compositional strengths of his commercial work, earned him over 100 awards. *Page 63, top left.*

Laurence Beverly Haste (1884-1954)

Although he produced a large body of commercial art work from 1910 to 1930, little is known about Haste's life and career. Born in San Francisco, he worked during the late teens and early 1920s at Shreve and Company. From the mid-1920s, he devoted himself full-time to his art, and was known as a talented illustrator and watercolorist. *Page 40 top left, 103 top, 122 left.*

George Heisley

Heisley, whose distinctive illustrations appeared on the covers of numerous publications in the 1920s, was active as a commercial artist in Los Angeles from circa 1908 to the 1930s. *Page 125, bottom right.*

Alfonso Iannelli (1888-1965)

Born in Italy, Iannelli came to United States as a child. He studied art at the Art Students League in New York. He is listed in Los Angeles Directories in the teens and from 1911 to 1913, he was an instructor at the Los Angeles Sketch Club. Sometime after 1915, he moved to Chicago. *Page 71, top left.*

Paul J. Immel (1896-1964)

Born in Montana, Immel moved to Los Angeles in 1924 to study at the Otis Art Institute. He worked in Los Angeles for only a short time. He spent the majority of his career in Seattle. *Page 163, top right.*

Lee C. Jennings

Jennings, born in Massachusetts, moved to California in 1908. While living in northern California for a short time, he worked for the Schmidt Lithograph Company. He settled in Los Angeles after World War I. *Page 4.*

Pedro Lemos (1882-1954)

Lemos was born in Nevada but grew up in Oakland. He studied art under Arthur Mathews at the Mark Hopkins Art Institute, then continued his studies at the Art Students in New York City, at Columbia, and in Chicago. Despite small inconsistencies between various sources, it is clear that Lemos developed a wide-ranging career in all areas of the visual arts. From 1902 to 1906, he was art director at several publishing houses and eventually managed the firm, Lemos Brothers Illustrators and Engravers. During this period he produced elegant illustrations for brochures and other ephemeral publications. He was also Professor of Design at the University of California from 1913 to 1914, and Head of the Design Department at the San Francisco Institute of Art from 1914 to 1916. From 1917 to 1945, he served as Director of the Museum of Fine Arts at Stanford University. His greatest artistic accomplishment was in the area of printmaking; he was one of the organizers of the California Society of Etchers. His work in several media was exhibited at several important venues including the Pennsylvania Academy of Fine Arts, the Corcoran Art Gallery, the Chicago Art Institute and at the Panama-Pacific International Exposition. *Page 40, bottom left.*

Maurice George Logan (1886-1977)

Logan, one of the most talented artists to produce work for promotional brochures, was born in San Francisco (according to most accounts) and grew up in Oakland. He received extensive formal training at the San Francisco Institute of Art from 1907 to 1913. He continued his studies at the Chicago Art Institute and the College of Arts and Crafts in Berkeley. It was about this time that Logan began working and exhibiting with "The Society of Six," a group of artists dedicated to modernist attitudes and individuality in their work. Although they employed distinctive styles, they shared a vision of truthfulness and directness in their *plein air* painting. Logan produced remarkable work during this period, roughly 1917 through 1927. He was also successful as a commercial artist, and was a founding partner in the firm Logan, Cox and Carey which later became Logan, Staniford and Cox, Commercial Illustrators. His clients included chambers of commerce, the San Francisco Visitors Bureau, Sunkist Advertising, Southern Pacific, and *Sunset Magazine*. His work in the 1920s was characterized by a bright, bold palette, which by the 1930s, evolved to more subdued tones. Also in the 1930s, he began to work in watercolor. His portrayal of the San Francisco Bay, Oakland Estuary and Alameda, as well as scenes beyond the Bay Area, elevated the quality of his commercial views above those produced by his contemporaries. He eschewed a decorative approach and avoided cliche. Distinctive as well as emulated, his commercial work in opaque watercolor or gouache, was probably the finest produced in the 1920s and 1930s. In 1933, he taught portrait and *plein air* painting at the Academie of Advertising Art in San Francisco. From 1935 to 1944, he taught at the College of Arts and Crafts. He also belonged to the Bohemian Club. For many years, he maintained an office on Sansome Street in San Francisco and lived in Oakland. *Page 26 bottom left, 64 top right, 65, 68 bottom left, 69 right, 70 bottom left, 80 left, 111 right, 113 right, 115, 117 right.*

George Frederick Mannel (1874-1961)

Born in Germany, Mannel immigrated with his family to California in 1885, when he was eleven years of age. Mannel, who was a successful commercial artist, lived and worked for most of his life in San Francisco. *Page 8 bottom detail, 31 right, 129 top left.*

Isabel C. Martin

Martin was a draftsman for the architectural design firm of E.P. Parcher at the time she was commissioned to produce the cover for *Hollywood, California* for the Hollywood Business Women's Club in 1922. Her name does not appear in Directories beyond the late 1920s. *Page 88, top.*

Earl Motter (1882-1965)

Motter lived and worked in San Diego in the 19-teens. At some later time, he settled in Sacramento where he continued his commercial art career. Sacramento Directories of the mid-1930s list Motter as co-owner of Alta Engraving. *Page 2, (Romance of California).*

Edward M. Muse (1874-1944)

Muse lived in Sacramento for thirty-five years and spent most of his career as a "delineator" for the State Division of Highways. In 1927, he developed designs for a Memorial Arch to California Pioneers for Capitol Park. Although the proposed monument was never realized, the design concept revealed Muse's interest in large-scale works and his skill in interpreting both contemporary and historical events through classical motifs and allegorical figures. *Page 145.*

Claude George Putnam, Sr. (1884-1955)

Putnam, who worked as a cartographer and commercial artist, was also an avid yachtsman. He wrote and illustrated several books including *Log Book, Harbors and Islands*, and *California Coast*. Putnam maintained a balance of his dual interests and careers. He was a member of the Commercial Artists Association of Southern California, and at the time of his death, he was also senior staff commodore of the Newport Harbor Yacht Club. *Page 97.*

Art Rasmussen

Rassmussen was a prolific commercial artist who lived and worked in Fresno from 1912 to 1940. Unfortunately, little else is known about this talented artist today. *Page 74, top left.*

Marea Ruocco

Ruocco's name appears in the 1930 San Diego Directory as an artist for the San Diego Chamber of Commerce, and for the next few years as a commercial artist. She may not have continued her artistic career beyond this period. *Page 155, right.*

Harold von Schmidt (1893-1982)

Born in Alameda and orphaned at age five, von Schmidt was raised by his grandfather who had been a "49er." His grandfather's stories and the works of Remington and Russell first inspired von Schmidt to study art. He began his training at the California College of Arts and Crafts, then continued for three years at the San Francisco Art Institute (as it is known today), and finally studied privately with Maynard Dixon and Worth Ryder. In 1924, von Schmidt moved to New York City and studied with the well-known illustrator Harvey Dunn. He developed his reputation as an illustrator of western subjects for the *Saturday Evening Post* and *Colliers*. From 1930, he lived and worked in Westport, Connecticut where he co-founded the Famous Artists School. Reflecting his childhood influences, von Schmidt produced twelve paintings of the 1849 Gold Rush for the California State Capitol. In 1960, he was commissioned to design a postage stamp commemorating the Pony Express. *Page 130, left.*

Paul Schmidt (1893-1983)

This successful illustrator and muralist was born in Philadelphia. At age 10, Schmidt and his parents, who had emigrated from Germany, moved to San Francisco. During his teens, he worked as a sign painter before embarking on art studies at the California School of Arts and Crafts in Berkeley. He exhibited at the Oakland Art Gallery in the late 1920s and early 1930s and at the Golden Gate International Exposition in 1939. He was also co-founder of the Society of Western Artists. This versatile artist, adept in several media, was in great demand as an illustrator. He solicited work as an aviation artist through an ad placed in a 1929 brochure, *Air Travel Guide*, for which he also produced the cover design. *Page 131, top left.*

Lloyd A. Schmucker

Although Schmucker's listing as a commercial artist appears in Los Angeles Directories of the 1930s, little other reliable information is available on this artist whose work appears on the covers of several chamber of commerce publications. *Page 74 top right, 161 bottom left.*

David Francis Schwartz (1879-1969)

Schwartz was born in Paris, Kentucky, and studied art at several institutions including the Art Institute of Chicago, and schools in Dayton, Cleveland and Montreal. Early in his career, he worked as an illustrator for the *Cleveland Plain Dealer*. In 1903, he moved to southern California and was employed as an illustrator for the *Los Angeles Times*. By 1915, he abandoned commercial art work to devote himself to fine art. In 1924, he was summoned to San Francisco to oversee installation of an 18 x 600-foot relief map of California in the Ferry Building. He maintained a studio at that location for 30 years. From this period, he produced paintings of northern California landscapes and missions, as well as portrait commissions. *Page 90, 91.*

Christian Siemer (1874-1940)

Siemer, a painter, illustrator and muralist, was born in New Zealand. In 1906, he emigrated to Los Angeles where he lived and worked for the remainder of his life. Los Angeles Directories of the mid-1930s listed him as an artist for the Los Angeles Chamber of Commerce. *Page 58, top right, 160 top left.*

Irving Sinclair (1895-1969)

Sinclair was born in British Columbia and in 1917, moved to San Francisco where he pursued a commercial art career. He worked in the art department of Foster and Kleiser and then, as art director for Fox West Coast Theatres. In 1939, he went to New York to study art. He returned to San Francisco to live, but continued to spend most of his summers in his native Canada. *Page 150, right.*

Langdon Smith (1870-1959)

Although born in Massachusetts, Smith moved first to Denver, then Pasadena, as a young boy. He studied at the Los Angeles School of Art and Design before taking a job as an illustrator for the *New York Herald* in 1895. After two years there, he returned to California. He pursued an active career as a commercial artist in Los Angeles, and produced numerous covers for chamber of commerce brochures and such publications as *West Coast Magazine*. From 1915, Langdon Smith divided his time between his Los Angeles studio during the winter months, and northern California for the balance of the year, where he enjoyed painting and recreational gold mining. *Page 61, top left.*

Arthur A. Vaillancourt (1888-1940)

There is little reliable biographical information on this talented Ohio-born illustrator. He is known to have moved to southern California in 1910 and to have been a member of the Commercial Artists of Southern California. Although Arthur Vaillancourt lived in Pasadena, he was listed as a commercial artist in Los Angeles Directories during the 1920s. *Page 56, top left.*

Hernando Villa (1881-1952)

Villa, whose parents were from Baja, California, was born in Los Angeles. He received support and encouragement from his mother who was a singer, and his father who was an artist. Villa studied at the Los Angeles School of Art and Design, and in England and Germany. He later taught at the School of Art and Design. He established his career as a commercial artist in Los Angeles by 1905. In 1915, he earned a Gold Medal for his mural at the Panama-Pacific International Exposition. He is best known for designing *The Chief*, the emblem of the Santa Fe Railroad Company for whom he worked for 40 years.

Ruth Taylor White

White, a successful cartoonist and commercial artist, lived and worked in San Francisco from 1928 to 1934. Little else is known today about her training or other interests. *Page 123, right.*

Raymond P. Winters

Little information is available on Winters. Los Angeles Directories confirm that he was active from the early 1920s to mid-1930s. In addition to chamber of commerce publications, he produced a number of covers for *Westways Magazine. Page 55, top.*

Jack Wisby (1870-1940)

Wisby, born in London, emigrated to San Francisco in 1897. There he married Mary Anne Fossey, an artist, and worked at Shreve's as an engraver. He made frequent sketching trips to the picturesque regions of Yosemite and Tahoe. Like so many others, Wisby lost his studio and most his artwork in the 1906 earthquake and fire. He then relocated to Marin County. In addition to his commercial work, Wisby produced evocative landscape views of northern California. *Page 71, bottom left.*

Edward Withers

Withers was born in New Zealand, and studied art in New Zealand, London and Paris before emigrating to southern California. A successful artist, he exhibited frequently, earned several awards, and was also President of the California Art Club. According to Los Angeles Directories, he worked as a commercial artist for Charles Ray Productions in the 1920s. Withers was active in Los Angeles to at least the early 1940s. *Page 54, 119 bottom left.*

Evelyn (Eva) Almond Withrow (1858-1928)

Withrow, whose image of a golden poppy graces the 1904 promotional booklet, *Land of Promise*, was a prominent artist in early 20th-century San Francisco. Born in Santa Clara, she was raised in San Francisco. After graduating from the College of the Pacific, she traveled to Europe with her mother. There, she studied art for four years in Munich. For the next seven years she lived in Paris. She and her sister moved to London where their home became the meeting place for artistic and literary leaders of the day. One of her great admirers, George Wharton James, referred to her as *a true California artist* and once commented on her ability to evoke *pastorale California*. He showcased her also in an article, *Evelyn Almond Withrow, Painter of the Spirit*, which appeared in the August 1916 issue of *National Magazine*. When she returned to San Francisco, Withrow established a *salon* in her family home. As further evidence of her prominence, Withrow was elected the first president of the San Francisco Society of Women Artists in 1925. She moved to San Diego the following year. *Page 162, top right.*

Ralph O. Yardley (1878-1961)

Yardley, who was born in Stockton, studied art in San Francisco at the Mark Hopkins Art Institute. In 1898, he was hired as a sketch artist for the *San Francisco Examiner*. In 1900, he was working in Hawaii and by 1905, in New York City. From there, he returned to San Francisco to work, for a short time, at the *Call*. Known as a painter and cartoonist, Directories confirm that Yardley returned to his hometown in 1921, where he worked for the next 30 years as a cartoonist for the *Stockton Record*. He was also known for paintings such as his view of Stockton which appears on a 1923 chamber of commerce brochure. *Page 83, right.*

Acknowledgments

All artwork marked with the initials CSL is from the collection of the California State Library, Sacramento, California. Artwork not so marked is from private collections. Dates beneath brochures and posters are intended to provide a time perspective. Many pieces were intentionally undated by their authors, often so that the piece could be used in successive years and in varied formats. At times, the same artwork was used as a poster, brochure cover and advertisement. Inconsistencies in production runs of some promotional literature sometimes resulted in interesting variants to the examples shown here. Original printed material in this book has been digitally reproduced. In some cases discolorations, creases, tears and other minor defects have been eliminated.

Artworks reproduced in this book are copyrighted by their respective owners (where applicable) and are used for historical and scholarly illustrative purposes. Reasonable effort has been made to identify copyright holders of works that might not be in the public domain.

Notes:

Page 1, postcard detail, 1910.

Page 2, background illustration, *Standard Oil Bulletin* cover detail by Maynard Dixon, 1929.

Page 4, Los Angeles County brochure detail, 1925.

Page 8, *bottom*, *Motor Land* cover detail, 1926.

Page 18-19, Edw. E. Eitel, Publisher, circa 1889.

Page 26, *top right*, advertisement, *Sunset*, 1914.

Page 27, *bottom right*, from Southern Pacific brochure, "Winter's Summer Garden," 1915.

Page 29, *bottom left*, advertisement, *Sunset*, 1905.

Page 30, *top right*, from *Motor Land* cover, 1927.

Page 32, *left*, advertisement, *Sunset*, 1902.

Page 33, *top left*, advertisement, *Sunset*, 1903.

Page 35, *top left*, inside page from "Sunset Limited" brochure.

Page 40, *top right*, inside page, brochure "Sunny Southern California."

Page 44, poster.

Page 47, *top right*, from brochure, "Butte County," 1912.

Page 56, *bottom*, from brochure, "Long Beach," circa 1920.

Page 57, *top left*, from *Sunset*, 1912.

Page 69, *right*, advertisement, *Sunset*, 1919.

Page 73, *bottom*, from "Pictorial History of the Aqueduct," 1913.

Page 75, poster

Page 80, *right*, from brochure, "Petaluma," circa 1913.

Page 81, *bottom left*, from *Sunset*, 1914.

Page 83, *bottom left*, inside pages, "Stockton," 1915.

Page 86, from "The San Diego Tourist," 1909

Page 88, background photo, Hollywoodland real estate development, 1923.

Page 93, *bottom and right*, from brochure, "Venice, California," 1922; *top*, from "Los Angeles and Picturesque Vicinity," 1914.

Page 96, *top left*, advertisement detail, *Scribners Magazine*, 1915.

Page 103, *bottom right*, from Southern Pacific brochure, "California for the Tourist," 1922.

Page 105, *right*, *Sunset*, 1916.

Page 108, *bottom left*, from *Sunset*, 1903; *right*, from "Souvenir Snapshots of Southern California," circa 1908.

Page 109, *right*, from "The Alexandria, Los Angeles," n.d.; *bottom*, photo by William H. Fletcher.

Page 113, *bottom left*, detail, *Standard Oil Bulletin* cover, 1915, *far right*, poster.

Page 114, *bottom left*, from *Sunset*, 1915.

Page 115, *top left*, *San Francisco Newsletter*, 1916; *bottom left* brochure detail, 1925.

Page 118, background photo, Avalon, Catalina Island, n.d.

Page 124, *left*, from *Sunset*, 1915.

Page 127, *bottom*, detail from "See California And All The West."

Page 128, *top left*, advertisement, *Sunset*, 1927; *bottom left*, from *Motor Land*, 1927; *bottom right*, from *Motor Land*, 1928; *top right*, advertisement, Tournament of Roses supplement, 1920.

Page 129, *top left*, from Motor Land cover, 1926.

Page 130, *bottom right*, inside page, "Los Angeles County," circa 1931.

Page 136-137, from CSL postcard collection.

Page 138, background photo, Panama-Pacific International Exposition, 1915.

Page 140, *far left*, poster.

Page 141, *left*, from *Sunset*, 1916; *right*, from *Sunset*, 1916.

Page 142, *far left*, poster.

Page 143, all posters.

Page 145, poster.

Page 155, *bottom left*, advertisement from Tournament of Roses supplement, 1931.

Page 161, *top left*, photo by William H. Fletcher.

Page 163, *center*, California State flag.

Bibliography

BOOKS

Baur, John E. *Health Seekers of Southern California, 1870 - 1900.* San Marino: Huntington Library, 1959.

Boas, Nancy. *The Society of Six: California Colorists.* San Francisco: Bedford Arts, 1988.

Chase, J. Smeaton. *Our Araby: Palm Springs and the Garden of the Sun.* Pasadena: Star-News Publishing Co., 1920.

Dawdy, Doris O. *A Biographical Dictionary, Volumes I, II, III.* Chicago: Sage Books, The Swallow Press Inc., 1974, 1981, 1985.

Dumke, Glenn S. *The Boom of the Eighties in Southern California.* San Marino: Huntington Library, 1970.

Hagerty, Donald J. *Desert Dreams: The Art and Life of Maynard Dixon.* Layton, Utah: Gibbs-Smith Publisher, 1993.

Elias, Judith W. *Los Angeles: Dream to Reality, 1885 - 1915.* Northridge: Santa Susana Press, 1983.

Hughes, Edan Milton. *Artists in California, 1786-1940.* San Francisco: Hughes Publishing Company, 1986 and 1989.

Irwin, Inez Haynes. *The Californiacs.* San Francisco: A.M. Robertson, 1916.

Jackson, Helen Hunt. *Ramona, a Story.* Boston: Little, Brown and Company, 1900 and other editions (first edition, Roberts Brothers, 1884).

James, George Wharton. *California Romantic and Beautiful.* Boston: The Page Company, 1914.

Kurutz, Gary F. *Benjamin C. Truman: California Booster and Bon Vivant.* San Francisco: The Book Club of San Francisco, 1984.

Kurutz, Gary F. *California Pastorale: Selected Photographs 1860 - 1925.* Sausalito: Windgate Press, 1998.

Marchand, Roland. *Advertising the American Dream: Making Way for Modernity, 1920 - 1940.* Berkeley and Los Angeles: University of California Press, 1985.

Markham, Edwin. *California the Wonderful.* New York: Hearst's International Library Co., 1914.

McClelland, Gordon T. and Last, Jay T. *California Orange Box Labels, an Illustrated History.* Beverly Hills: Hillcrest Press, 1985.

Moure, Nancy Dustin Wall. *Dictionary of Art and Artists in Southern California before 1930, Publications in Southern California. Volume 3.* Los Angeles: Dustin Publications, 1984.

Moure, Nancy Dustin Wall. *Loners, Mavericks, Dreamers: Art in Los Angeles before 1900.* Laguna Beach: Laguna Art Museum, 1993.

Murphy, Thomas D. *On Sunset Highways, a Book of Motor Rambles in California.* Boston: The Page Company, 1915, Revised 1921.

Murphy, Thomas D. *Three Wonderlands of the American West.* Boston: L.C. Page & Co., 1912.

Neuhaus, Eugen. *The Art of Treasure Island.* Berkeley: University of California Press, 1939.

Nordoff, Charles. *California: For Health, Pleasure and Residence, a Book for Travellers and Settlers.* New York: Harper & Brothers, Publishers, 1872.

Orsi, Richard J. *Selling the Golden State; A Study of Boosterism in Nineteenth-Century California.* Unpublished Doctoral Dissertation, University of Wisconsin, Madison, 1973.

Page, Henry Markham. *Pasadena: Its Early Years.* Los Angeles: Lorrin L. Morrison Printing and Publishing, 1964.

Perine, Robert. *Chouinard, An Art Vision Betrayed.* Encinitas: Artra Publishing, 1985.

Runte, Alfred. *Trains of Discovery: Western Railroads and the National Parks.* Niwot, Colorado: Roberts Rinehart, Inc., Revised Edition, 1990.

Sanders M.D., F.C.S. *California as a Health Resort.* San Francisco: Bolte & Braden Co., 1916.

Starr, Kevin. *Inventing the Dream: California through the Progressive Era.* New York: Oxford University Press, 1985.

Starr, Kevin. *Material Dreams: Southern California through the 1920s.* New York: Oxford University Press, 1990.

Truman, Maj. Ben C. *Homes and Happiness in the Golden State of California.* San Francisco: Passenger Department, Central Pacific Railroad Company, 1883.

Truman, Maj. Ben C. *Semi-Tropical California.* San Francisco: A.L. Bancroft & Co., 1874.

Warner, Charles Dudley. *Our Italy.* New York: Harper and Brothers, 1891.

Westphal, Ruth Lilly, editor. *Plein Air Painters of California: The North.* Irvine: Westphal Publishing, 1986.

Westphal, Ruth Lilly. *Plein Air Painters of California: The Southland.* Irvine: Westphal Publishing, 1982.

Willard, Charles Dwight. *A History of the Chamber of Commerce of Los Angeles, California From its Foundation, September, 1888 to the Year 1900.* Los Angeles: Kingsley-Barnes & Neuner Co., 1899.

OTHER PRIMARY SOURCES

Artists Biographical Files; California State Library, California History Section.

California City Directories. California State Library; Various, based on accessible editions.

PROMOTIONAL BROCHURES AND PAMPHLETS
Credited by Author(s)

Benton, F. Weber. *Venice of America, California, All Year.* Los Angeles: Benton Publishing Company, 1922.

Bitler, Don C., Editor. *Imperial Valley, California, America's Amazing Winter Garden.* El Centro: Board of Supervisors of Imperial Valley, March 1, 1920.

Chipman, N.P. *California, the Land of Promise.* San Francisco: The California State Board of Trade, 1904.

Brook, Harry Ellington. *The Land of Sunshine: Southern California.* Los Angeles: World's Fair Association and Bureau of Information, 1893.

Estee, M.M. Address at Citrus Fair. Sacramento, December 14, 1886.

Forbes, Mrs. A.S.C. *California Mission and Landmarks and How to Get There.* Los Angeles: State Federation of Women's Clubs, 1903.

French, Harold. *Siskiyou County, California.* The Board of Supervisors and The Panama-Pacific International Exposition Commission of Siskiyou County, 1915.

Holder, Charles Frederick. *A Climatic Miracle in California*. Chicago: Passenger Department, The Santa Fe, 1903.

Nicholson, George T. *The California Limited, 1903-1904*. Chicago: Santa Fe Railroad Company; 1903.

Truman, Maj. Ben C. *Tourists Illustrated Guide to the Celebrated Summer and Winter Resorts of California*. San Francisco: H.S. Crocker & Co., 1883.

Wells, A.J. *Contra Costa County, California*. San Francisco: Sunset Homeseekers's Bureau, 1910.

Wells, A.J. *Irrigation: California, Nevada, Oregon, Arizona*. San Francisco: Passenger Department Southern Pacific, 1910.

Uncredited / Anonymous Authors

(The) Alexandria. Los Angeles: c. 1920s.

California for the Settler. San Francisco: Southern Pacific Company, 1917 and other editions.

California: The Opening Gun in California's Advertising Campaign. San Francisco: Californians, Inc., c. 1921.

California, Winter's Summer Garden. Chicago: Chicago, Milwaukee & St. Paul Railway, 1915.

Claremont: A Private Residence Park at Berkeley. Berkeley and San Francisco: Mason-McDuffie Company and Oakland: R.S. Ritchener, c. 1910.

Coming to California? Fresno: Fresno Chamber of Commerce, c. 1908.

Curry's Lebec Lodge on the Ridge Route. c. 1930s.

Citrus Exhibition, Fifth Annual, Held at Riverside, California, March 14, 15 and 16, 1883, Proceedings of Semi-Annual State Convention of Fruit Growers. Riverside: Press and Horticulturist Steam Print, 1883.

(The) Frostless Belt. Anaheim: Board of Trade, 1915.

Fullerton, Orange County. Fullerton: Chamber of Commerce with the City of Fullerton, c. 1923.

Golden Gate Bridge Fiesta, San Francisco. San Francisco: Golden Gate Bridge and Highway District, Redwood Empire Association and the City and County of San Francisco, 1937.

Greater Sacramento: Her Achievements, Resources and Possibilities. Sacramento: Sacramento Chamber of Commerce, 1912.

Hollywood, California. Hollywood: Hollywood Business Women's Club, 1922.

Hotel Oakland, The Crossroads of the Air. n.d.

Let's Go Places, California State Parks and Historic Monuments. Richfield Oil Company of California. Chicago: The H. M. Grousha Company, 1935.

Los Angeles County. Los Angeles: Board of Supervisors of Los Angeles County, c. 1940.

(The) Mission Play by John Steven McGroarty. Los Angeles: Smith-Barnes Corporation, various editions.

(The) Ontario-Cucamonga-Etiawanda Colonies, The Banner Fruit District of Southern California. North Ontario: Ontario-Cucamonga-Etiwanda Fruit Exchange, San Bernadino County, 1902

Orland, The Project of No Regrets. U.S. Government Irrigation Project, Glenn County. Orland: Chamber of Commerce, c. 1922.

(The) Raymond-Whitcomb Tours to California and the Expositions in 1915. Boston: Raymond and Whitcomb Company, 1914.

Richardson Mineral Springs. (Butte County) San Jose: Rosicrucian Press, 1936.

Richmond, The Pittsburg of the West. Richmond: Richmond Chamber of Commerce, 1907.

Second Annual Citrus Fair of the San Gabriel Valley to be Held at Pasadena, March 3rd to 6th Inclusive. N.P., 1883.

Souvenir of Southern California Orange Carnival, April 1891. Chicago: State Citrus Fair Committee of Southern California, 1891.

Sunny Southern California. Los Angeles: Chamber of Commerce of Los Angeles, c. 1925 and other editions.

Thermalito Colony: The Pasadena of Central California. [Butte County] 1887.

Treasure Island on San Francisco Bay, Golden Gate International Exposition. San Francisco: Southern Pacific Lines, 1938.

Vacation Land, The Playground of California. San Francisco: Northwestern Pacific Railway, c. 1915.

Wawona Hotel: 4000 Feet above Sea Level. Wawona, Mariposa County: Wawona Hotel Company, and San Francisco: The Peck-Judah Co., c. 1920s.

What Can Be Done for Humboldt County. Eureka: Humboldt Promotion and Development Committee, 1912.

Where California Fruits Grow: Resources of Sacramento County: A Souvenir of The Bee. Sacramento: James McClatchy & Co., 1894, Second Edition 1895.

(The) Wonder City, Los Angeles, El Pueblo de Nuestra Senora, La Reina de Los Angeles, 1781-1931. Los Angeles: Charles P. Grossman, 1931.

Yosemite: California's All-Year Playland. Yosemite Park: Yosemite Park and Curry Co., 1926.

Books illustrated on Pages 12, 13, 14, 15, and 135, not listed in the Bibliography.

Austin, Mary. *California, The Land of the Sun*. Painted by Sutton Palmer. New York: The Macmillan Company, 1914.

Chase, James Smeaton. *Yosemite Trails*. Boston and New York: Houghton Mifflin and Company, 1911.

Clements, Edith S. *Flowers of Coast and Sierra*. New York: The H.W. Wilson Co., 1928.

Forbes, A.S.C. *Mission Tales in the Days of the Dons*. Los Angeles: Gem Publishing Co., 1926. *(Page 135)*

Hutchinson, W.E. *Byways Around San Francisco Bay*. New York and Cincinnati: The Abingdon Press, 1915.

Peixotto, Ernest. *Romantic California*. New York: Charles Scribner's Sons, 1910.

Jackson, Helen Hunt. *Ramona*. Boston: Little, Brown, and Company, 1900. *(Page 135)*

James, George Wharton. *The Lake of the Sky, Lake Tahoe*. New York: J.F. Tapley Co., 1915.

James, George Wharton. *Exposition Memories, San Diego 1916*. Pasadena: Radiant Life Press, 1917.

Muir, John. *My First Summer in the Sierra*. Boston and New York: Houghton Mifflin and Company, 1911

Saunders, Charles Francis. *With Flowers and Trees in California*. New York: Robert M. McBride & Co.,1923.

Saunders, Charles Frances. *Under the Sky in California*. New York: Robert M. McBride & Co., 1926.

PLACE NAME INDEX